CONGRESSIONAL OVERSIGHT

CONGRESSIONAL OVERSIGHT

Martin O. James (Ed.)

Nova Science Publishers, Inc.
New York

Senior Editors: Susan Boriotti and Donna Dennis
Coordinating Editor: Tatiana Shohov
Office Manager: Annette Hellinger
Graphics: Wanda Serrano
Editorial Production: Jennifer Vogt, Matthew Kozlowski and Maya Columbus
Circulation: Ave Maria Gonzalez, Indah Becker, Raymond Davis and Vladimir Klestov
Communications and Acquisitions: Serge P. Shohov
Marketing: Cathy DeGregory

Library of Congress Cataloging-in-Publication Data
Available Upon Request

ISBN 1-59033-301-2

Copyright © 2002 by Nova Science Publishers, Inc.
      400 Oser Ave, Suite 1600
      Hauppauge, New York 11788-3619
      Tele. 631-231-7269   Fax 631-231-8175
      e-mail: Novascience@earthlink.net
      Web Site: http://www.novapublishers.com

Printed in the United States of America

CONTENTS

PREFACE

Throughout its history, Congress has engaged in oversight of the executive branch-the review, monitoring, and supervision of the implementation of public policy. The first several Congresses inaugurated such important oversight techniques as special investigations, reporting requirements, resolutions of inquiry, and use of the appropriations process to review executive activity. Contemporary developments, moreover, have increased the legislature's capacity and capabilities to check on and check the Executive. Public laws and congressional rules have measurably enhanced Congress's implied power under the Constitution to conduct oversight. Despite its lengthy heritage, oversight was not given explicit recognition in public law until enactment of the Legislative Reorganization Act of 1946. That act required House and Senate standing committees to exercise "continuous watchfulness" over programs and agencies within their jurisdiction. Since the late 1960s Congress has shown increasing interest in oversight for several major reasons. These include the expansion in number and complexity of federal programs and agencies; increase in expenditures and personnel, including contract employees; rise (until recently) in the budget deficit; and the frequency of divided government, with Congress and the White House controlled by different parties. Major partisan disagreements over priorities and processes also heighten conflict between the legislature and the executive.

Oversight occurs in virtually any congressional activity and through a wide variety of channels, organizations, and structures. These range from formal committee hearings to informal Member contracts with executive officials, from staff studies to support agency reviews, and from casework conducted by Member offices to studies prepared by non-congressional entities, such as statutory commissions and offices of inspector general.

I. PURPOSES, AUTHORITY, AND PARTICIPANTS

Throughout its history, Congress has engaged in oversight of the executive branch the review, monitoring, and supervision of the implementation of public policy. The first several Congresses inaugurated such important oversight techniques as special investigations, reporting requirements, resolutions of inquiry, and use of the appropriations process to review executive activity. Contemporary developments, moreover, have increased the legislature's capacity and capabilities *to check on and check the Executive*. Public laws and congressional rules have measurably enhanced Congress's implied power under the Constitution to conduct oversight.

Despite its lengthy heritage, oversight was not given explicit recognition in public law until enactment of the Legislative Reorganization Act of 1946. That act required House and Senate standing committees to exercise *"continuous watchfulness"* over programs and agencies within their jurisdiction.

Since the late 1960s, according to such scholars as political scientist Joel Aberbach, Congress has shown increasing interest in oversight for several major reasons. These include the expansion in number and complexity of federal programs and agencies; increase in expenditures and personnel, including contract employees; rise (until recently) in the budget deficit; and the frequency of divided government, with Congress and the White House controlled by different parties. Major partisan disagreements over priorities and processes also heighten conflict between the legislature and the executive.

Oversight occurs in virtually any congressional activity and through a wide variety of channels, organizations, and structures. These range from formal committee hearings to informal Member contacts with executive officials, from staff studies to support agency reviews, and from casework conducted by Member offices to studies prepared by noncongressional entities, such as statutory commissions and offices of inspector general.

PURPOSES

Congressional oversight of the Executive is designed to fulfill a number of purposes:

A. Ensure Executive Compliance with Legislative Intent

Congress, of necessity, must delegate discretionary authority to federal administrators. To make certain that these officers faithfully execute laws according to the intent of Congress, committees and Members can review the actions taken and regulations formulated by departments and agencies.

B. Improve the Efficiency, Effectiveness, and Economy of Governmental Operations

A large federal bureaucracy makes it imperative for Congress to encourage and secure efficient and effective program management, and to make every dollar count toward the achievement of program goals. Many federal programs can be improved through better managerial operations and service delivery. Such steps can strengthen the accountability of agency managers to Congress and enhance program performance.

C. Evaluate Program Performance

Systematic program performance evaluation remains a relatively new and still-evolving technique in oversight. Modem program evaluation uses social science and management methodologies, such as surveys, cost-benefit analyses, and efficiency studies, to assess the effectiveness of ongoing programs.

D. Prevent Executive Encroachment on Legislative Prerogatives and Powers

Beginning in the late 1960s, many commentators, public policy analysts, and legislators argued that Presidents and executive officials overstepped their authority in various areas such as impoundment of funds, executive privilege, war powers, and the dismantling of federal programs without congressional consent. Increased oversight as part of the checks and balances system was called for to redress what many in the public and Congress saw to be an executive arrogation of legislative prerogatives.

E. Investigate Alleged Instances of Poor Administration, Arbitrary and Capricious Behavior, Abuse, Waste, Dishonesty, and Fraud

Instances of fraud and other forms of corruption, the breakdown of federal programs, incompetent management, and the subversion of governmental processes arouse legislative and public interest in oversight.

F. Assess Agency or Officials' Ability to Manage and Carry Out Program Objectives

Congress's ability to evaluate the capacity of agencies and managers to carry out program objectives can be accomplished in various ways. For example, numerous laws require agencies to submit reports to Congress; some of these are regular, occurring annually or semi-annually, for instance, while others are activated by a specific event, development, or set of conditions. The report requirement may promote self-evaluation by the agency. Organizations outside of Congress, such as offices of inspector general and study commissions, also advise Members and committees on how well federal agencies are working.

G. Review and Determine Federal Financial Priorities

Congress exercises some of its most effective oversight through the appropriations process, which provides the opportunity to review recent expenditures in detail. In addition, most federal agencies and programs are under regular and frequent reauthorizations on an annual, two-year, four-year, or other basis giving the authorizing committees the same opportunity. As a consequence of these oversight efforts, Congress can abolish or curtail obsolete or ineffective programs by cutting off or reducing funds or it may enhance effective programs by increasing or earmarking funds.

H. Ensure that Executive Policies Reflect the Public Interest

Congressional oversight can appraise whether the needs and interests of the public are adequately served by federal programs, and thus lead to corrective action, either through legislation or administrative changes.

I. Protect Individual Rights and Liberties

Congressional oversight can help to safeguard the rights and liberties of citizens and others. By revealing abuses of authority, for instance, oversight hearings can halt executive misconduct and help to prevent its recurrence, either directly through new legislation or indirectly by putting pressure on the offending agency.

J. Other Specific Purposes

The general purposes of oversight and what constitutes this function can be stated in more specific terms. Like the general purposes, these unavoidably overlap because of the numerous and multifaceted dimensions of oversight. A brief list includes:

1. review the agency rulemaking process;

2. monitor the use of contractors and consultants for government services;

3. encourage and promote mutual cooperation between the branches;

4. examine agency personnel procedures;

5. acquire information useful in future policymaking;

6. investigate constituent complaints and media critiques;

7. assess whether program design and execution maximize the delivery of services to beneficiaries;

8. compare the effectiveness of one program with another;

9. protect agencies and programs against unjustified criticisms; and

10. study federal evaluation activities.

Thoughts on Oversight and its Rationale from . . .

James Wilson *(The Works of James Wilson,* 1896, vol. II, p. 29), an architect of the Constitution and Associate Justice on the first Supreme Court:

> The house of representatives.., form the grand inquest of the state. They will diligently inquire into grievances, arising both from men and things.

Woodrow Wilson *(Congressional Government,* 1885, p. 297), perhaps the first scholar to use the term "oversight" to refer to the review and investigation of the executive branch:

> Quite as important as legislation is vigilant oversight of administration.

> It is the proper duty of a representative body to look diligently into every affair of government and to talk much about what it sees. It is meant to be the eyes and the voice, and to embody the wisdom and will of its constituents.

> The informing function of Congress should be preferred even to its legislative function.

John Stuart Mill *(Considerations on Representative Government,* 1861, p. 104). British utilitarian philosopher:

> the proper office of a representative assembly is to watch and control the government; to throw the light of publicity on its acts; to compel a full exposition and justification of all of them, which any one considers questionable...

AUTHORITY TO CONDUCT OVERSIGHT

A. United States Constitution

The Constitution grants Congress extensive authority to oversee and investigate executive branch activities. The constitutional authority for Congress to conduct oversight stems from such explicit and implicit provisions as:

1. *The power of the purse.* The Constitution provides that "No Money shall be drawn from the Treasury, but in Consequence of Appropriations made by Law." Each year the Committees on Appropriations of the House and Senate review the financial practices and needs of federal agencies. The appropriations process allows the Congress to exercise extensive control over the activities of executive agencies. Congress can define the precise purposes for which money may be spent, adjust funding levels, and prohibit expenditures for certain purposes.

2. *The power to organize the executive branch.* Congress has the authority to create, abolish, reorganize, and fund federal departments and agencies. It has the authority to

assign or reassign functions to departments and agencies, and grant new forms of authority and staff to administrators. Congress, in short, exercises ultimate authority over executive branch organization and policy.

3. *The power to make all laws for "carrying into Execution "Congress's own enumerated powers as well as those of the executive.* Article 1 grants Congress a wide range of powers, such as the power to tax and coin money; regulate foreign and interstate commerce; declare war; provide for the creation and maintenance of armed forces; and establish post offices. Augmenting these specific powers is the so-called "Elastic Clause," which gives Congress the authority "To make all Laws which shall be necessary and proper for carrying into Execution the foregoing Powers, and all other Powers vested by this Constitution in the Government of the United States, or in any Department or Officer thereof." Clearly, these provisions grant broad authority to regulate and oversee departmental activities established by law.

4. *The power of impeachment, removal, and confirmation.* Impeachment offers Congress a powerful tool to investigate alleged executive (and judicial) misbehavior, and to eliminate such behavior through the conviction and removal from office of the offending individual. The confirmation process not only involves the determination of a nominee's suitability for an executive (or judicial) position, but also provides an opportunity to examine the current policies and programs of an agency along with those policies and programs that the nominee intends to pursue.

5. *The power of investigation and inquiry.* A traditional method of exercising the oversight function, an implied power, is through investigations and inquiries into executive branch operations. Legislators need to know how effectively and efficiently programs are working, how well agency officials are responding to legislative directives, and how the public perceives the programs. The investigatory method helps to ensure a more responsible bureaucracy, while supplying Congress with information needed to formulate new legislation.

The Supreme Court on Congress's Power to Oversee and Investigate

McGrain v. *Daugherty,* 273 U.S. 135, 177, and 181-182 (1927):

> Congress, investigating the administration of the Department of Justice during the Teapot Dome scandal, was considering a subject "on which legislation could be had or would be materially aided by the information which the investigation was calculated to elicit." The "potential" for legislation was sufficient. The majority added, "We are of [the] opinion that the power of inquiry—with the process to enforce it—is an essential and appropriate auxiliary to the legislative function."

Eastland v. United States Servicemen's Fund, 421 U.S. 491, 509 (1975):

> Expanding on its holding in McGrain, the Court declared, "To be a valid legislative inquiry there need be no predictable end result."

B. Principal Statutory Authority

A number of laws directly augment Congress's authority, mandate, and resources to conduct oversight, including assigning specific duties to committees. Among the most important, listed chronologically, are:

1. *1912 Anti-Gag Legislation and Whistleblower Protection Laws for Federal Employees*

   a. The 1912 Act countered executive orders, issued by Presidents Theodore Roosevelt and William Howard Taft, which prohibited civil service employees from communicating directly with Congress.

   b. It also guaranteed that "the right of any persons employed in the civil service... to petition Congress, or any Member thereof, or to furnish information to either house of Congress, or to any committee or member thereof, shall not be denied or interfered with." 37 Stat. 555 (1912) codified at 5 U.S.C. 7211 (1994).

   c. The Whistleblowers Protection Act of 1978, as amended, makes it a prohibited personnel practice for an agency employee to take (or not take) any action against an employee that is in retaliation for disclosure of information that the employee believes is in violation of law, rule or regulation or which evidences gross mismanagement, waste, fraud or abuse of authority (5 U.S.C. 2302 (b) (8)). The prohibition is explicitly intended to protect disclosures to Congress:

   d. "This subsection shall not be construed to authorize the withholding of information from the Congress or the taking of any personnel action against an employee who disclosures information to the Congress.

   e. Intelligence Community Whistleblower Protection Act (P.L. 105-272) establishes special procedures for personnel in the Intelligence Community, to transmit urgent concerns involving classified information to inspectors generals and the House and Senate Select committees on intelligence.

2. *1921 Budget and Accounting Act Establishing the General Accounting Office (GAO)*

   a. insisted that GAO "shall be independent of the executive departments and under the control and direction of the Comptroller General of the United States." (Emphasis added.) 42 Stat. 23 (1921)

   b. Granted authority to the Comptroller General to "investigate, at the seat of government or elsewhere, all matters relating to the receipt, disbursement, and application of public funds." (Emphasis added.) 42 Stat. 26 (1921)

3. *1946 Legislative Reorganization Act*

    a. Mandated House and Senate committees to exercise "continuous watchfulness "of the administration of laws and programs under their jurisdiction. (Emphasis added.) 60 Stat. 832 (1946)

    b. Authorized for the first time in history, permanent professional and clerical staff for committees. 60 Stat. 832 (1946)

    c. Authorized and directed the Comptroller General to make administrative management analyses of each executive branch agency. 60 Stat. 837 (1946)

    d. Established the Legislative Reference Service, renamed the Congressional Research Service by the 1970 Legislative Reorganization Act (see below), as a separate department in the Library of Congress and called upon the Service "to advise and assist any committee of either House or joint committee in the analysis, appraisal, and evaluation of any legislative proposal ... and otherwise to assist in furnishing a basis for the proper determination of measures before the committee." (Emphasis added.) 60 Stat. 836 (1946)

4. *1968 Intergovernmental Cooperation Act*

    a. Required that House and Senate committees having jurisdiction over grants-in-aid are to conduct studies of the programs under which grants-in-aid are made. 82 Stat. 1098 (1968)

    b. Provided that these studies are to determine whether: (1) their purposes have been met, (2) their objectives could be carried on without further assistance, (3) they are adequate to meet needs, and (4) any changes in programs or procedures should be made. 82 Stat. 1098 (1968)

5. *1970 Legislative Reorganization Act*

    a. Revised and rephrased in more explicit language the oversight function of House and Senate standing committees: ". . . each standing committee shall review and study, on a continuing basis, the application, admin is/ration, and execution of those laws or parts of laws, the subject matter of which is within the jurisdiction of that committee." (Emphasis added.) 84 Stat. 1156 (1970)

    b. Required most House and Senate committees to issue biennial oversight reports. 84 Stat. 1156 (1970)

    c. Strengthened the program evaluation responsibilities and other authorities and duties of the General Accounting Office. 84 Stat. 1168-1171 (1970)

d. Redesignated the Legislative Reference Service as the Congressional Research Service, strengthening its policy analysis role and expanding its other responsibilities to Congress. 84 Stat. 1181-1185 (1970)

e. Recommended that House and Senate committees ascertain whether programs within their jurisdiction could be appropriated for annually. 84 Stat. 1174-1175(1970)

f. Required most House and Senate committees to include in their committee reports on legislation jive-year cost estimates for carrying out the proposed program. 84 Stat. 1173-1174(1970)

g. Increased by two the number of permanent staff/breach standing committee, including provision minority party hirings, and provided for hiring of consultants by standing committees. 84 Stat. 1175-1179(1970)

6. *1972 Federal Advisory Committee Act*

a. Directed House and Senate committees to make a continuing review of the activities of each advisory committee under its jurisdiction. 86 Stat 771 (1972)

b. The studies are to determine whether: (1) such committee should be abolished or merged with any other advisory committee, (2) its responsibility should be revised, and (3) it performs a necessary function not already being performed. 86 Stat. 771(1972) (Advisory committee charters and reports can generally be obtained from the agency or government being advised.)

7. *1974 Congressional Budget Act, as Amended*

a. *Expanded* House and Senate committee *authority for oversight.* Permitted committees to appraise and evaluate programs themselves "or by contract, or (to) require a Government agency to do so and furnish a report thereon to the Congress." 88 Stat. 325 (1974)

b. Directed the comptroller general to *review and evaluate the results of Government programs and activities* ", on his own initiative, or at the request of either House or any standing or joint committee and to assist committees in analyzing and assessing program reviews or evaluation studies. (Emphasis added.) Authorized GAO to establish an Office of Program Review and Evaluation to carry out these responsibilities. 88 Stat. 326 (1974)

c. Strengthened GAO's role in *acquiring fiscal, budgetary, and program-related information.* 88 Stat. 327-329 (1974)

d. Required any House or Senate legislative committee report on a public bill or resolution to include an *analysis* (prepared by the Congressional Budget Office) providing an *estimate and comparison of costs* which would be incurred in carrying out the bill during the next and following four fiscal years in which it would be effective. 88 Stat. 320 (1974)

e. Established House and Senate Budget Committees and the Congressional Budget Office. The CBO director is authorized to *"secure information, data, estimates, and statistics directly* from the various departments, agencies, and establishments" of the government. 88 Stat. 302 (1974)

8. *Other Noteworthy Statutory Provisions*

Separate from expanding its own authority and resources directly, Congress has strengthened its oversight capabilities *indirectly*, by, for instance, establishing study commissions to review and evaluate programs, policies, and operations of the government. In addition, Congress has created various *mechanisms, structures, and procedures within the executive* that improve the executive's ability to monitor and control its own operations and, at the same time, provide additional information and oversight-related analyses to Congress. These statutory provisions include:

a. Establishing offices of inspector general in all cabinet departments, larger agencies and numerous boards, commissions, and government corporations *Inspector General Act of 1978*, as amended, 5 U.S.C. Appendix 3

b. Establishing chief financial officers in all cabinet departments and larger agencies *Chief Financial Officers Act of 1990*, 107 Stat. 2838 (1990)

c. Improving the efficiency, effectiveness, and equity in the exchange of funds between the federal government and state governments *Cash Management Improvement Act of 1990*, 104 Stat. 1058 (1990)

d. Increasing efficiency, effectiveness, and accountability within the government *Government Performance and Results Act of 1993*, 107 Stat. 285-296 (1993)

e. Improving the executive's stewardship of federal resources and accountability *Government Management and Reform Act of 1994*, 108 Stat. 3410 (1994)

f. Controlling federal paperwork requirements *Paperwork Reduction Act of 1995*, 109 Stat. 163 (1995)

g. Establishing the position of chief information officer in federal agencies to provide relevant advice for purchasing the best and most cost-effective information technology available *Information Technology Improvement Act*, 110 Stat. 679 (1996)

h. Improving the government's ability to manage its programs *Federal Managers' Financial Integrity Act of 1982*, 96 Stat. 814-815 (1982)

i. Establishing uniform audit requirements for state and local governments and nonprofit organizations receiving federal financial assistance *Single Audit Act of 1984,* as amended, 98 Stat. 2327 (1984) and 110 Stat. 679 (1996)

j. Creating a mechanism by which congress can review and disapprove virtually any federal rule or regulation *Small Business Regulatory Enforcement Fairness Act of 1996,* 110 Stat. 857-874 (1996)

C. Responsibilities in House and Senate Rules

1. House Rules

   a. House rules grant the Committee on Government Reform a broad role in oversight activities (Rule X, clause 4). For example, pertinent review findings and recommendations of this committee are to be considered by the authorizing committees, if presented to them in a timely fashion. In addition, the authorizing committees are to indicate on the cover of their reports on public measures that they contain a summary of such findings when that is the case (Rule XII, clause 3).

   b. The Committee on Government Reform has additional oversight duties to:

      (1) review and study on a continuing basis, the operation of government activities at all levels to determine their economy and efficiency (Rule X, clause 3);

      (2) receive and examine reports of the comptroller general and submit recommendations thereon to the House (Rule X, clause 4);

      (3) evaluate the effects of laws enacted to reorganize the legislative and executive branches of the government (Rule X, clause 4);

      (4) study intergovernmental relationships between the United States and states, municipalities, and international organizations of which the United States is a member (Rule X, clause 4); and

      (5) *report an oversight agenda,* not later than March 31 of the first session of a Congress, based upon oversight plans submitted by each standing committee and after consultation with the Speaker of the House, the majority leader, and the minority leader. The oversight agenda is to include the oversight plans of each standing committee together with any recommendations that it or the House leadership group may make to ensure the most effective coordination of such plans (Rule X, clause 2).

   c. House rules mandate or provide authority for other oversight efforts by *standing committees:*

(1) Each standing committee (except Appropriations and Budget) shall review and study on a continuing basis the application, administration, and execution of all laws within its legislative jurisdiction (Rule X, clause 2).

(2) Committees have the authority to review the impact of tax policies on matters that fall within their jurisdiction (Rule X, clause 2).

(3) Each committee (except Appropriations and Budget) has a responsibility for futures research and forecasting (Rule X, clause 2).

(4) Specified committees have special oversight authority, i.e., the right to conduct comprehensive reviews of specific subject areas that are within the legislative jurisdiction of other committees. Special oversight is akin to the broad oversight authority granted the Committee on Government Reform, by the 1946 Legislature Reorganization Act, except that special oversight is generally limited to named subjects (Rule X, clause 3).

(5) Each standing committee is authorized to require its subcommittees, if any, to conduct oversight in their jurisdictional areas or to create an oversight subcommittee; a committee that establishes such a subcommittee may add it as a sixth subcommittee, beyond the usual limit of five (Rule X, clauses 2 and 5).

(6) Committee reports on measures are to include oversight findings separately set out and clearly identified (Rule XIII, clause 3).

(7) Costs of stenographic services and transcripts for oversight hearings are to be paid "from the applicable accounts of the house" (Rule XI, clause 1).

(8) Each standing committee is to submit its oversight plans for the duration of a Congress by February 15 of the first session to the Committee on Government Reform and the Committee on House Administration. Not later than March 31, the Government Reform Committee must report an oversight agenda (discussed above), in developing such plans, each standing committee must, to the extent feasible (Rule X, clause 2):

(a) consult with other committees of the House that have jurisdiction over the same or related laws, programs, or agencies within its jurisdiction, with the objective of ensuring that such laws, programs, or agencies are reviewed in the same Congress and that there is a maximum of coordination between such committees in the conduct of such reviews; and such plans shall include an explanation of what steps have been and will be taken to ensure such coordination and cooperation;

(b) give priority consideration to including in its plans the review of those laws, programs, or agencies operating under permanent budget authority or permanent statutory authority; and

(c) have a view toward ensuring that all significant laws, programs, or agencies within its jurisdiction are subject to review at least once every 10 years.

(9) *Each committee* must submit to the house, not later than January 2 of each odd-numbered year, *a report on the activities of that committee* for the Congress (Rule XI, clause 1):

(a) Such report must include *separate sections summarizing the legislative and oversight activities* of that committee during that Congress.

(b) The *oversight section* of such report must include a summary of the oversight plans submitted by the committee at the beginning of the Congress, a summary of the actions taken and recommendations made with respect to each such plan, and a summary of any additional oversight activities undertaken by that committee, and any recommendations made or actions taken thereon.

d. *The Speaker,* with the approval of the House, is given additional authority to "appoint *special ad hoc oversight committees* for the purpose or reviewing specific matters within the jurisdiction of two or more standing committees." (Emphasis added.) (Rule X, clause 2)

2. *Senate Rules*

a. Each standing committee (except for Appropriations and Budget) must review and study on a continuing basis, the application, administration, and execution of all laws within its legislative jurisdiction (Rule XXVI, clause 8).

b. "Comprehensive policy oversight" responsibilities are granted to specified standing committees. This duty is similar to special oversight in the House. The Committee on Agriculture, Nutrition, and Forestry, for example, is authorized to "study and review, on a comprehensive basis, matters relating to food, nutrition, and hunger, both in the United States and in foreign countries, and rural affairs, and report thereon from time to time (Rule XXV, clause 1a)."

c. All standing committees, except Appropriations, are required to prepare regulatory impact evaluations in their committee reports accompanying each public bill or joint resolution (Rule XXVI, clause 11). The evaluations arc to include:

(1) an estimate of the numbers of individuals and businesses to be affected;

(2) a determination of the regulation's economic impact and effect on personal privacy; and

(3) a determination of the amount of additional paperwork that will result.

d. The Committee on Governmental Affairs has the following additional oversight duties (Rule XXV, clause 1k):

(1) review and study on a continuing basis the operation of government activities at all levels to determine their economy and efficiency;

(2) receive and examine reports of the comptroller general and submit recommendations thereon to the Senate;

(3) evaluate the effects of laws enacted to reorganize the legislative and executive branches of the government; and

(4) study intergovernmental relationships between the United States and states, municipalities, and international organizations of which the United States is a member.

CONGRESSIONAL PARTICIPANTS IN OVERSIGHT

A. Members and Committees

1. *Members.* Oversight is generally considered a committee activity. However, both casework and other project work conducted in a Member's personal office can result in findings about bureaucratic behavior and policy implementation; these, in turn, can lead to the adjustment of agency policies and procedures and to changes in public law.

   (a) *Casework* responding to constituent requests for assistance on projects or complaints or grievances about program implementation provides an opportunity to examine bureaucratic activity and operations, if only in a selective way.

   (b) Sometimes *individual Members* will conduct their own investigations or *ad hoc* hearings, or direct their staffs to conduct oversight studies. Individual Members have no authority to issue compulsory process or conduct official hearings. The General Accounting Office or some other legislative branch agency, a specially created task force, or private research group might be requested to conduct an investigation of a matter for a Senator or Representative.

2. *Committees.* The most common and effective method of conducting oversight is through the committee structure. Throughout their histories, the House and Senate have used their standing committees as well as select or special committees to investigate federal activities and agencies along with other matters.

(a) The House Committee on *Government Reform* and the Senate Committee on *Governmental Affairs,* which have oversight jurisdiction over virtually the entire federal government, have been vested with broad investigatory powers over governmentwide activities.

(b) The House and Senate Committees on *Appropriations* have similar responsibilities when reviewing fiscal activities.

(c) Each *standing* committee of Congress has oversight responsibilities to review government activities within their jurisdiction. These panels also have authority on their own to establish oversight and investigative *subcommittees.* The establishment of such subcommittees does *not preclude* the *legislative* subcommittees from conducting oversight.

(d) Certain House and Senate committees have *"special oversight"* or *"comprehensive policy oversight"* of designated subject areas as explained in the previous subsection.

B. Staff of Member Offices and Committees

1. *Personal staff.* Constituent letters, complaints, and requests for projects and assistance frequently bring problems and deficiencies in federal programs and administration to the attention of Members and their personal office staffs. The casework performed by a Member's staff for constituents can be an effective oversight tool.

   (a) Casework can be an important vehicle for pursuing both the oversight and legislative interests of the Member. The Senator or Representative and the staff may be attuned to the *relationship* between *casework* and the *oversight* function. This is facilitated by a regular exchange of ideas among the Member, legislative aides, and caseworkers on problems brought to the office's attention by constituents, and of possible legislative initiatives to resolve those problems.

   (b) If casework is to be useful as an oversight technique, *effective staffing and coordination are critical.* Casework and legislative staffs maximize service to their Member's constituents when they establish a relationship with the staff of the subcommittees and committees that handle the areas of concern to the Member's constituents. Through this interaction, the panel's staff can be made aware of the problems with the agency or program in question, assess how widespread and significant it is, determine its causes, and recommend corrective action.

   (c) *Office procedures* enable staff in some offices to identify cases that represent a situation in which forma/ changes in agency procedure could be an appropriate remedy. Prompt congressional inquiry and follow up enhance this type of oversight. Telephone inquiries reinforced with written requests tend to ensure agency action.

2. *Committee Staff.* As issues become more complex and Members' staffs more overworked, professional staffs of committees can provide the expert help required to conduct oversight and investigations. Committee staff typically have the experience and expertise to conduct effective oversight for the committees and subcommittees they serve. Committees may also call upon *legislative support agencies* for assistance, hire *consultants,* or *"borrow" staff* from federal departments.

Committee staff, in summary, occupy a central position in the conduct of oversight. The informal contacts with executive officials at all levels constitute one of Congress's most effective devices for performing its "continuous watchfulness" function.

C. Congressional Support Agencies and Offices

1. Of the agencies in the legislative branch, three directly assist Congress in support of its oversight function (See Section V. below for further detail on each):

   (a) Congressional Budget Office (CBO),

   (b) Congressional Research Service (CRS) of the Library of Congress, and

   (c) General Accounting Office (GAO).

2. Additional offices that can assist in oversight are:

   (a) House General Counsel's Office,

   (b) Senate Legal Counsel's Office, and

   (c) Senate Historian's Office and Senate Library.

SELECTED READINGS

Aberbach, Joel D. Keeping a Watchful Eye: The Politics of Congressional Oversight. Washington: Brookings Institution, 1990.

JK585.A63

Congressional Oversight: Methods and Techniques. Committee Print, Prepared for the Subcommittee on Oversight Procedures of the Senate Committee on Government Operations by the Congressional Research Service and the General Accounting Office, 94th Cong., 2d sess. Washington: GPO, 1976.

Ehlke, Richard. Congressional Access to Information From the Executive: A Legal Analysis. CRS Report 86-50A, March 10, 1986.

Fisher, Louis. Constitutional Conflicts between Congress and the President, Lawrence, Kansas: University Press of Kansas, 1997, 4th Revised Edition.

KF4565.F57

Foreman, Christopher H. Signals from the Hill: Congressional Oversight and the Challenge of Social Regulation. New Haven: Yale University Press, 1988.

JK585.F68

Harris, Joseph P. Congressional Control of Administration, Washington: Brookings Institution. 1964.

JKIO6I.H3

History of the United States House of Representatives, 1789-1994. H. Doe. 103-324, 1 03d Cong., 2d sess. Washington: GPO, 1994. Chapter XI, "Oversight," pp. 233-266.

Kaiser, Frederick M. Congressional Oversight. CRS Report 97-936 GOV, January 2, 2001.
_____ Congressional Oversight of the Presidency. Annals, vol. 499, September 1988, pp. 75-89.

Leading Cases on Congressional Investigatory Power (Compiled by the Joint Committee on Congressional Operations). Committee Print, 94th Cong., 2d sess. Washington: GPO, 1976.

Maskell, Jack H. and Morton Rosenberg. Congressional Intervention in the Administrative Process: Legal and Ethical Considerations. CRS Report 90-440A, September 7, 1990.

Mayhew, David R. Divided We Govern: Party Control, Lawmaking, and Investigations, 1946-1990. New Haven: Yale University Press, 1991.

JK2261.M36

McCubbins, Mathew D. and Thomas Schwartz. Congressional Oversight Overlooked: Police Patrol Versus Fire Alarms. American Journal of Political Science, vol. 2, February 1984, pp. 165-79.

National Academy of Public Administration. Panel on Congress and the Executive. Beyond Distrust: Building Bridges Between Congress and the Executive. Washington: NAPA, 1992.

Ogul, Morris S. Congress Oversees the Bureaucracy: Studies in Legislative Supervision. Pittsburgh: University of Pittsburgh Press, 1976.

JK585.048

Oleszek, Walter J. Congressional Procedures and the Policy Process Washington: Congressional Quarterly Press, 2001. Chapter 10, Legislative Oversight.

JKI 096.043

Rosenberg, Morton. Congress's Prerogative Over Agencies and Agency Decisionmakers: The Rise and Demise of the Reagan Administration's Theory of the Unitary Executive. George Washington Law Review, vol. 57, January 1989, pp. 627-703.

_____ Whatever Happened To Congressional Review of Rulemaking? A Brief Overview, Assessment and Proposal for Reform. Administrative Law Review, vol. 51, Fall 1999, pp. 1051-1092.

_____ Congressional Review of Agency Rulemaking: A Brief Overview and Assessment After Five Years. CRS Report RL3O1 16, March 6, 2001.

_____ Investigative Oversight: An Introduction to the Law, Practice and Procedure of Congressional Inquiry. CRS Report 95-464 A, April 7, 1995.

Rosenbloom, David H. Building a Legislative-Centered Public Administration: Congress and the Administrative State, 1946-1999. Tuscaloosa, Ala.: The University of Alabama Press, 2000.

KFT6OI .R58

Schlesinger, Arthur M. and Roger Bruns, eds. Congress Investigates: A Documented History, 1792-1974(5 vols.) New York: Chelsea House Publishers, 1975.

JKI 123.A2S34

Study on Federal Regulation: Congressional Oversight of Regulatory Agencies. Senate Doe. 95-26, 95th Cong., 1st sess. Washington: GPO, 1977.

U.S. General Accounting Office. Investigators Guide to Sources of Information. GAO Report OSI-97-2. Washington: GAO, 1997.

West, William F. Controlling the Bureaucracy: Institutional Constraints in Theory and Practice. Armonk, New York and London, England: M.E. Sharpe: 1995.

JK421 .W44

II. Oversight Coordination and Processes

A persistent problem for Congress in conducting oversight is coordination among committees, both within each chamber as well as between the two. As the final report of the House Select Committee on Committees of the 93rd Congress noted, "Review findings and recommendations developed by one committee are seldom shared on a timely basis with another committee, and, if they are made available, then often the findings are transmitted in a form that is difficult for Members to use." Despite the passage of time, this statement remains relevant today. Oversight coordination between House and Senate committees is also uncommon.

Intercommittee cooperation on oversight can prove beneficial for a variety of reasons. It should, for example, minimize unnecessary duplication and conflict and inhibit agencies from playing one committee off against another. There are formal and informal ways to achieve oversight coordination among committees.

Oversight Coordination

A. General Techniques of Ensuring Oversight Coordination Include

1. The House and Senate can establish select or special committees to probe issues and agencies, to promote public understanding of national concerns, and to coordinate oversight of issues that overlap the jurisdiction of several standing committees.

2. House rules require the findings and recommendations of the Committee on Government Reform to be considered by the authorizing committees if presented to them in a timely fashion. Such findings and recommendations are to be published in the authorizing committees' reports on legislation. House rules also require the oversight plans of committees to include ways to maximize coordination between and among committees that share jurisdiction over related laws, programs, or agencies.

B. Specific Means of Ensuring Oversight Coordination Include

1. Joint oversight hearings on programs or agencies.

2. Informal agreement among committees to oversee certain agencies and not others. For example, the House and Senate Committees on Commerce agreed to hold oversight hearings on certain regulatory agencies in alternate years.

3. Consultation between the authorizing and appropriating committees. For example, the two Committees on Commerce worked closely and successfully with their corresponding appropriations subcommittees to alert those panels to the authorizing committees' intent with respect to regulatory ratemaking by such agencies as the Federal Communication Commission.

OVERSIGHT PROCESSES

A. The Budget Process

1. The Congressional Budget and Impoundment Control Act of 1974, as amended, enhanced the legislative branch's capacity to shape the federal budget. The act has major institutional and procedural effects on Congress:

    a. *Institutionally,* Congress created three new entities:

        (1) the Senate Committee on the Budget;
        (2) the House Committee on the Budget; and
        (3) the Congressional Budget Office.

    b. *Procedurally,* the act established methods that permit Congress to:

        (1) determine budget policy as a whole;
        (2) relate revenue and spending decisions;
        (3) determine priorities among competing national programs; and
        (4) ensure that revenue, spending, and debt legislation is consistent with the overall budget policy.

2. The new budget process coexists with the older authorization and appropriation procedures and significantly affects each.

    a. On the *authorization side,* the Budget Act requires committees to submit their budgetary "views and estimates" for matters under their jurisdiction to their Committee on the Budget within six weeks after the President submits a budget.

    b. On the *appropriations side,* new contract and borrowing authority must go through the appropriations process. Subcommittees of the Appropriations

Committees are assigned a financial allocation that determines how much may be included in the measures they report, although less than one-third of federal spending is subject to the annual appropriations process. (The tax and appropriations panels of each house also submit budgetary views and estimates to their respective Committee on the Budget.)

c.   In deciding spending, revenue, credit, and debt issues, Congress is sensitive to trends in the overall composition of the annual federal budget (expenditures for defense, entitlements, interest on the debt, and domestic discretionary programs).

3.   In short, the Budget Act has the potential of strengthening oversight by enabling Congress better to relate program priorities to financial claims on the national budget. Each committee, knowing that it will receive a fixed amount of the total to be included in a budget resolution, has an incentive to scrutinize existing programs to make room for new programs or expanded funding of ongoing projects or to assess whether programs have outlived their usefulness.

B. The Authorization Process

1.   Through its authorization power, Congress exercises significant control over any government agency.

2.   The entire authorization process may involve a host of oversight tools hearings, studies, and reports but the key to the process is the *authorization statute.*

a.   An authorization statute creates and shapes government programs and agencies and it contains the statement of legislative policy for the agency.

b.   Authorization is the *first* lever in congressional exercise of the power of the purse; it usually allows an agency to be funded, but it does *not* guarantee financing of agencies and programs. Frequently, authorizations establish dollar ceilings on the amounts that can be appropriated.

3.   The authorization-reauthorization process is an important oversight tool.

a.   Through this process, Members are educated about the work of an agency and given an opportunity to direct the agency's effort in light of experience.

b.   Expiration of an agency's program provides an excellent chance for in-depth oversight:

(1) In recent decades, there has been a shift from permanent to periodic (annual or multi-year) authorizations, although some reformers are now pressing for *biennial budgeting* (acting on a two-year cycle for authorizations, appropriations, and budget resolutions).

(2) Periodic authorizations improve the likelihood that an agency will be scrutinized systematically.

4. In addition to formal amendment of the agency's authorizing statute, the authorization process gives committees an opportunity to exercise informal, nonstatutory controls over the agency.

   a. The knowledge by the agency that it must usually come to the legislative committee for renewed authority increases the influence of the committee.

   b. This condition helps to account for the trend to short-term authorizations.

   c. *Nonstatutory controls* used by committees to exercise direction over the administration of laws include statements made in:

      (1) committee hearings;
      (2) committee reports accompanying legislation; and
      (3) floor debates.

5. If agencies fail to comply with these informal directions, the authorization committees can apply sanctions and convert the informal direction into a statutory command.

C. The Appropriations Process

1. 1.The appropriations process is one of Congress's most important forms of oversight.

   a. Its strategic position stems from the constitutional requirement that "no Money shall be drawn from the Treasury, but in Consequence of Appropriations made by Law."

   b. Congress's power of the purse allows the House and Senate Committees on Appropriations to play a prominent role in oversight.

2. The oversight function of the Committees on Appropriations derives from their responsibility to examine and pass on the budget requests of the agencies as contained in the President's Budget.

   a. The decisions of the committees are conditioned on their assessment of the agencies' need for their budget request as indicated by past performance.

   b. In practice, the entire record of an agency is fair game for the required assessment.

   c. This comprehensive overview and the "carrot and stick" of the appropriations recommendations make the committees significant focal points of congressional oversight and is a key source of their power in Congress and in the federal government generally.

3. Enacted appropriations legislation frequently contains at least five types of *statutory controls* on agencies:

   a. Such legislation specifies the *purpose* for which funds may be used.

   b. It defines the specified funding *level* for the agency as a whole as well as for programs and divisions within the agency.

   c. It sets *time limits* on the availability of funds for obligation.

   d. Appropriations legislation may contain *limitation* provisions. For example, in appropriating $350 million to the Environmental Protection Agency for research and development, Congress added this condition: "Provided, That not more than $55,000,000 of these funds shall be available for procurement of laboratory equipment, supplies, and other operating expenses in support of research and development." 108 Stat. 2319 (1994).

   e. Appropriations measures also stipulate how an agency's budget can be *reprogrammed* (shifting funds within an appropriations account; see box below).

4. *Nonstatutory controls* are a major form of oversight. Legislative language in committee reports and in hearings, letters to agency heads, and other communications give detailed instructions to agencies regarding committee expectations and desires. Agencies are not legally obligated to abide by nonstatutory recommendations, but failure to do so is likely to result in a loss of funds and flexibility the following year. Agencies ignore nonstatutory controls at their peril (see box).

The conference report for the Omnibus Consolidated and Emergency Supplemental Appropriations for FY 1999 provides guidelines for the reprogramming and transfer of funds for the Treasury and General Government Appropriations Act, 1999. Each request from an agency to the review committee "shall include a declaration that, as of the date of the request, none of the funds included in the request have been obligated, and none will be obligated, until the Committees on Appropriations have approved the request." H. Rept. No. 105-825. p. 1472 (1998).

D. The Investigatory Process

1. Congress's power of investigation is *implied* in the Constitution.

   a. Numerous Supreme Court decisions have upheld the legislative branch's right of inquiry, provided it stays within its legitimate legislative sphere.

b. The roots of Congress's authority to conduct investigations extend back to the British Parliament and colonial assemblies.

c. In addition, the Framers clearly perceived the House of Representatives to function as a "grand inquest." Since the Framers expected lawmakers to employ the investigatory function, based upon parliamentary precedents, it was unnecessary to invest Congress with an explicit investigatory power.

d. From time to time, legal questions have been raised about the investigative authority of Congress. However, numerous Supreme Court decisions have upheld the legislative branch's right of inquiry, provided it stays within its legitimate legislative sphere.

2. Investigations and related activities may be conducted by:

a. individual Members;

b. committees and subcommittees;

c. staff or outside organizations and personnel under contract; or

d. congressional support agencies.

3. Investigations serve several purposes:

a. they help to ensure honesty and efficiency in the administration of laws;

b. they secure information that assists Congress in making informed policy judgments; and

c. they may aid in informing the public about the administration of laws.

[See Section III for greater detail and analysis]

E. The Confirmation Process

By establishing a public record of the policy views of nominees, congressional hearings allow lawmakers to call appointed officials to account at a later time. Since at least the Ethics in Government Act of 1978, which encouraged greater scrutiny of nominations, Senate committees are leaving more time to probing the qualifications, independence, and policy predilections of presidential nominees, seeking information on everything from physical health to financial assets. Confirmation can assist in oversight in several ways.

1. The Constitution provides that the President "shall nominate, and by and with the *Advice and Consent of the Senate,* shall appoint Ambassadors, other public Ministers and Consuls, Judges of the supreme court, and all other Officers of the United States,

whose Appointments are not herein otherwise provided for, and which shall be established by Law." (Emphasis added.)

   a. The consideration of appointments to administrative leadership positions is a major responsibility of the Senate and especially of Senate committees.

   b. Panels review the qualifications of nominees for public positions.

2. The confirmation hearing provides a forum for the discussion of the policies and programs the nominee intends to pursue; this is a classic opportunity for senatorial oversight and influence. The confirmation process as an oversight tool can be used to:

   a. provide policy direction to nominees;

   b. inform nominees of congressional interests; and

   c. extract future commitments.

3. Once a nominee has been confirmed by the Senate, oversight includes following up to ensure that the nominee fulfills the commitments made during confirmation hearings. Subsequent hearings and committee investigations can explore whether those commitments have been kept.

4. *Recess appointments.* The Construction provides that the President "shall have Power to fill up all Vacancies that may happen during the Recess of the Senate, by granting Commissions which shall expire at the End of their next Session." When Presidents relied on this power to circumvent Senate confirmation, Congress responded with legislation that prohibits, with certain exceptions, the payment of salaries to recess appointees, certain exceptions, the payment of salaries to recess appointees. 54 Stat. 751 (1940); 5 U.S.C. 5503 (1994). Also, in the annual Treasury-Postal Service Appropriations Act, Congress enacts an additional funding restriction on recess appointees (see box).

No part of any appropriation for the current fiscal year contained in this or any other Act shall be paid to any person for the filling of any position for which he or she has been nominated after the Senate has voted not to approve the nomination of said person. 114 Stat. 2763A-157, sec. 609 (2000).

---

5. *Vacancies Act.* In addition to making recess appointments, Presidents make other temporary or interim appointments. Since 1795, Congress has legislated limits on the time a temporary officer may occupy a vacant advice and consent position. In 1868, Congress established a procedure for filling vacancies in advice and consent positions through the Vacancies Act. When the head of an executive department dies, resigns, or is sick or absent, the next in command may perform the duties until a successor is appointed or the absence ceases. The President may also direct someone

else (previously appointed with the advice and consent of the Senate) to perform the duties. These acting officials, under the Vacancies Act, were restricted by law to a period of not to exceed 30 days. That limit was violated with such frequency that Congress in 1988 increased it to 120 days. 102 Stat. 988, sec. 7(1988); 5 U.S.C. 3345-48 (1994).

The Justice Department took the position that some executive officials were not restricted by the Vacancies Act and could serve beyond the 120-day period. Under that interpretation, the administration selected Bill Lann Lee to head the Justice Department's Civil Rights Division, and he could serve longer than had he been a recess appointee. Congress responded by passing legislation in 1998 to make the Vacancies Act the exclusive vehicle for temporarily filling vacant advice and consent positions. The new Vacancies Act, included in the FY 1999 Omnibus Consolidated and Emergency Supplemental Appropriations Act (P.L. 105-277), rejects the Justice Department position and established procedures for the appointment of executive officials who temporarily hold an office. With various exceptions, the 120-day period has been replaced by a 210-day period.

F. The Impeachment Process

1. The impeachment power of Congress is a unique oversight tool, reserved for unusual circumstances and as a technique of last resort when conventional forms fail. Impeachment applies also to the judiciary, but the focus here is on efforts by Congress to impeach executive officials. Impeachment offers Congress:

   a. a constitutionally mandated method for obtaining information that might otherwise not be made available by the executive; and

   b. an implied threat of punishment for an executive official whose conduct exceeds acceptable boundaries.

2. Impeachment procedures differ from those of conventional congressional oversight.

   a. The most significant procedural differences center on the *roles* played by each house of Congress.

   b. The House of Representatives has the sole power to impeach. A majority is required to impeach.

   c. If the House votes to impeach, the person is tried by the Senate, which has the sole power to try an impeachment. A two-thirds majority is required to convict and remove the individual. Should the Senate deem it appropriate in a given case, it may, by majority vote, impose an additional judgment of disqualification from further federal offices of honor, trust, or profit.

d. In *Nixon v. United States, 506* U.S. 226 (1993), the Supreme Court held nonjusticiable a constitutional challenge to the use by the Senate in an impeachment proceeding of a 12-member committee appointed to take testimony and gather evidence. Such a committee makes no recommendations as to the ultimate question before the Senate. Nor does the committee rule on questions of relevancy, materiality, and competency. Rather, it reports a certified copy of the transcript of the proceedings before the committee and any evidence received by the committee to the full Senate for its consideration. The full Senate may take further testimony or evidence, or it may hold the entire trial in open Senate. In either event, the full Senate determines whether to convict on one or more of the articles of impeachment involved and, upon conviction, decides the appropriate judgment to be imposed.

3. The impeachment process is cumbersome and infrequently used. The House has voted to impeach in only 17 cases, 16 of which have reached the Senate, and 15 of which have gone to a vote on one or more articles of impeachment. Seven cases, all pertaining to federal judges, have resulted in conviction and removal; two of these also resulted in disqualification. The most recent impeachment trial was that of President Clinton in 1998-99; the most recent judicial impeachment trials were those of Judges Claiborne, Hastings, and Nixon in 1986, 1988 and 1989, respectively. A number of issues were addressed in the Clinton impeachment trial and other past impeachment proceedings, although the answers to some still remain somewhat ambiguous. For example:

a. An impeachment may be continued from one Congress to the next, although the procedural steps vary depending upon the stage in the process.

b. The Constitution defines the grounds for impeachment as "Treason, Bribery, or other high Crimes and Misdemeanors." However, the meaning and scope of "high Crimes and Misdemeanors" remains in dispute and depends on the interpretation of individual legislators.

c. The Constitution provides for impeachment of the "President, Vice President, and all civil Officers of the United States." While the outer limits of the "civil Officers" language are not altogether clear, past precedents suggest that it covers at least federal judges and executive officers subject to the Appointments Clause. Members of the House and Senate are not subject to impeachment because they are not "civil officers."

SELECTED READINGS

The Budget Process

Fisher, Louis. Presidential Spending Power. Princeton, N.J.: Princeton University Press, 1975. 345 p.

HJ257.2.F57

Keith, Robert and Allen Schick. Manual on the Federal Budget Process. CRS Report No. 98-720 GOV, August 25, 1998.

Schick, Allen. Congress and Money. Washington, D.C.: Urban Institute, 1980. 604 p.

HJ2051.S34

Wilmerding, Lucius, Jr. The Spending Power: A History of the Efforts of Congress to Control Expenditures. New Haven, Conn.: Yale University Press, 1943. 317 p.

HJ2OI 3.U5W5

Authorization and Appropriation Processes

Devins, Neal E. "Regulation of Government Agencies Through Limitation Riders," Duke Law Journal, v. 1987, 1987:456.

Fisher, Louis. "Annual Authorizations: Durable Roadblocks to Biennial Budgeting," Public Budgeting & Finance, v. 3, Spring 1983: 24.

_____ "The Authorization-Appropriation Process in Congress: Formal Rules and Informal Practices," Catholic University Law Review, v. 29, 1979: 51.

Fenno, Richard F., Jr. The Power of the Purse. Boston, Mass.: Little, Brown, 1966. 704 p.

JK 1074.F4

LeBoeuf, Jacques B. "Limitations on the Use of Appropriations Riders by Congress to Effectuate Substantive Policy Changes," Hastings Constitutional Law Quarterly, v. 19, Winter 1992: 457.

LeLoup, Lance T. "Appropriations Politics in Congress: The House Appropriations Committee and the Executive Agencies," Public Budgeting & Finance, v. 4, Winter 1984: 78.

U.S. General Accounting Office, Office of General Counsel. Principles of Federal Appropriations Law. Vols. I, II, and 111, 1991, 1994.

The Investigatory Process [See Section III]

The Confirmation Process

Carter, Stephen L. The Confirmation Mess: Cleaning Up the Federal Appointments Process. New York: Basic Books, 1994. 252p.

JK736.C37

Fisher, Louis. Recess Appointments of Federal Judges. CRS Report No. RL3 112, September 5, 2001.

Gerhardt, Michael J. The Federal Appointments Process. Durham and London: Duke University Press, 2000. 400 p.

JK73 I .G47

_____ "Toward a Comprehensive Understanding of the Federal Appointments Process," Harvard Journal of Law and Public Policy, v. 21, no. 4, 1998: 468.

Harris, Joseph P. The Advice and Consent of the Senate: A Study of the Confirmation of Appointments by the United States Senate. Berkeley, Cal.: University of California Press, 1953. 457 p.

JK1274.H3

Haynes, George H. The Senate of the United States: Its History and Practice. Boston, Mass.: Houghton Mifflin Co., 1938. 2 vols. 1118 p.

JK1161.H28

Kim, Haeryon. "Congressional Influence on the FCC: An Analysis of Confirmation Hearings for Commission Chairmen, 1969-1989," Communications and the Law, v. 15, 1993: 37.

Mackenzie, C. Calvin. The Politics of Presidential Appointments. New York: The Free Press, 1981, 298 p.

JK736.M33

Rosenberg, Morton. The New Vacancies Act: Congress Acts to Protect the Senate's Confirmation Prerogative. CRS Report No. 98-892A, November 2, 1998.

Ross, William C. "The Senate's Constitutional Role in Confirming Cabinet Nominees and Other Executive Officials," Syracuse Law Review, vol. 48, 1998: 1123.

The Impeachment Process

Bazan, Elizabeth B. Impeachment: An Overview of Constitutional Provisions, Procedure, and Practice. CRS Report 99-186 A, February 27, 1998.

Black, Charles L., Jr. Impeachment: A Handbook. New Haven, Conn.: Yale University Press, 1974. 80 p. LC 73-923 15

Bushnell, Eleanor. Crimes, Follies, and Misfortunes: The Federal Impeachment Trials. Urbana, Ill.: University of Chicago Press, 1992. 380 p.

KF8781.B87

Gerhardt, Michael J. The Federal Impeachment Process: A Constitutional and [Historical Analysis. Princeton, N.J.: Princeton University Press, 1996. 2133p.

KF4958.G47

Labowitz, John R. Presidential Impeachment. New Haven: Yale University Press,1978. 257 p.

KF5075.L33

Maskell, Jack. Censure of the President by the Congress. CRS Report No. 98-343A, December 8, 1998.

Posner, Richard A. An Affair of State: The Investigation, Impeachment, and Trial of President Clinton. Cambridge, Mass.: Harvard University Press, 1999. 276 p.

KF5 076. C5 7P67

Rehnquist, William H. Grand Inquests: The Historic Impeachments of Justice Samuel Chase and President Andrew Johnson. New York: William Morrow and Co., 1992. 303p.

E302.6C4R44

U.S. Congress. "Impeachment: Selected Materials," Committee on the Judiciary, House of Representatives, 93d Cong., 1st Sess., October 1973. 718 p.

_____ "Impeachment: Selected Materials on Procedure," Committee on the Judiciary, House of Representatives, 93d Cong., 2d Sess., January 1974. 900 p.

_____ "Constitutional Grounds for Impeachment: Modem Precedents," Committee on the Judiciary, House of Representatives, 105th Cong., 2d Sess., Ser. No.9, November 1998. 94 p.

_____ "Impeachment: Selected Materials," Committee on the Judiciary, House of Representatives, 105th Cong., 2d Sess., Ser. No. 10, November 1998. 1854 p.

III. INVESTIGATIVE OVERSIGHT

Congressional investigations, often adversarial and confrontational, sustain and vindicate Congress's role in our constitutional scheme of separated powers. The rich history of congressional investigations, from the failed St. Clair expedition in 1792 through Teapot Dome, Watergate, Iran-Contra, and Whitewater, has established, in law and practice, the nature and contours of congressional prerogatives necessary to maintain the integrity of the legislative role in that constitutional scheme.

This section provides a brief overview of some of the more common legal, procedural, and practical issues that committees face in the course of an investigation. Following a summary of the case law developing the scope and limitations of the power of inquiry, the essential tools of investigative oversight subpoenas, staff interviews and depositions, grants of immunity, and the contempt power are described. Next, some of the special problems of investigating the executive branch are detailed, with particular emphasis on claims of presidential executive privilege and agency assertions of common law testimonial privileges. The section concludes with a discussion of the role of the minority in the investigatory process.

A. THE LEGAL BASIS FOR OVERSIGHT

Numerous Supreme Court precedents recognize a broad and encompassing power in Congress to engage in oversight and investigation that would reach all sources of information necessary for carrying out its legislative function. In the absence of a countervailing constitutional privilege or a self-imposed statutory restriction upon its authority, Congress and its committees have plenary power to compel information needed to discharge its legislative function from executive agencies, private persons, and organizations. Within certain constraints, the information so obtained may be made public.

Although there is no express provision of the Constitution that specifically authorizes Congress to conduct investigations and take testimony for the purposes of performing its legitimate functions, numerous decisions of the Supreme Court have firmly established that the investigatory power of Congress is so essential to the legislative function as to be implied from the general vesting of legislative power in Congress.[1] Thus, in *Eastland v. United States*

---

[1] McCrain v. Daugherty, 272 U.S. 135 (1927).

Servicemen's Fund, the Court explained that "[t]he scope of its power of inquiry . . . is as penetrating and far-reaching as the potential power to enact and appropriate under the Constitution."[2] In *Watkins v. United States,* the Court described the breadth of the power of inquiry: "The power of the Congress to conduct investigations is inherent in the legislative process. That power is broad. It encompasses inquiries concerning the administration of existing laws as well as proposed or possibly needed statutes."[3] The Court went on to emphasize that Congress's investigative power is at its peak when the subject is alleged waste, fraud, abuse, or maladministration within a government department. The investigative power, it stated, "comprehends probes into departments of the Federal Government to expose corruption, inefficiency, or waste."[4]

But while the congressional power of inquiry is broad, it is not unlimited. The Supreme Court has admonished that the power to investigate may be exercised only "in aid of the legislative function"[5] and cannot be used to expose for the sake of exposure alone. The *Watkins* Court underlined these limitations: "There is no general authority to expose the private affairs of individuals without justification in terms of the functions of the Congress. . . nor is the Congress a law enforcement or trial agency. These are functions of the executive and judicial departments of government. No inquiry is an end in itself; it must be related to, and in furtherance of, a legitimate task of the Congress."[6] Moreover, an investigating committee has only the power to inquire into matters within the scope of the authority delegated to it by its parent body.[7] But once having established its jurisdiction and authority and the pertinence of the matter under inquiry to its area of authority, a committee's investigative purview is substantial and wide-ranging.

B. THE TOOLS OF OVERSIGHT

1. The Subpoena Power

The power of inquiry, with the accompanying process to enforce it, has been deemed "an essential and appropriate auxiliary to the legislative function."[8] A properly authorized subpoena issued by a committee or subcommittee has the same force and effect as a subpoena issued by the parent House itself. To validly issue a subpoena, individual committees or subcommittees must be delegated this authority. Senate Rule XXVI(1) and House Rule XI(2)(m)(1) presently empower all standing committees and subcommittees to require the attendance and testimony of witnesses and the production of documents. Special or select committees must be specifically delegated that authority by Senate or House resolution. The rules or practices of standing committees may restrict the issuance of subpoenas only to full

---

[2] 421 U.S. at 504, n. 15 (quoting *Barenblatt v. United States,* 360 U.S. 109, 111).
[3] 354 U.S. 178, 187 (1957).
[4] *Id.*
[5] *Kilbourn v. Thompson,* 103 U.S. 168, 204 (1880).
[6] *Watkins v. United States,* 354 U.S. at 187.
[7] *United States v. Rumely,* 345 U.S. 41, 42, 44 (1953); *Watkins v. United States,* 354 U.S. at 198.
[8] *McGrain v. Daughtery,* 273 U.S. at 174-75.

committees or in certain instances allow issuance by a committee chairman alone, with or without the concurrence of the ranking minority member.[9]

Congressional subpoenas are most frequently served by the U.S. marshal's office or by committee staff, or less frequently by the Senate or House sergeants-at-arms. Service may be effected anywhere in the United States. The subpoena power reaches aliens in the United States. Securing compliance of United States nationals and aliens living in foreign countries presents more complex problems.

A witness seeking to challenge the legal sufficiency of a subpoena has only limited remedies to raise objections. The Supreme Court has ruled that courts may not enjoin the issuance of a congressional subpoena, holding that the Speech or Debate Clause of the Constitution[10] provides "an absolute bar to judicial interference" with such compulsory process.[11] As a consequence, a witness's sole remedy generally is to refuse to comply, risk being cited for contempt, and then raise the objections as a defense in a contempt prosecution.

Challenges to the legal sufficiency of subpoenas must overcome formidable judicial obstacles. The standard to be applied in determining whether the congressional investigating power has been properly asserted was articulated in *Wilkinson v. United States:*[12] (1) the committee's investigation of the broad subject matter area must be authorized by Congress; (2) the investigation must be pursuant to "a valid legislative purpose"; (3) and the specific inquiries must be pertinent to the broad subject matter areas which have been authorized by the Congress. As to the requirement of "valid legislative purpose," the Supreme Court has made it clear that Congress does not have to state explicitly what it intends to do as a result of an investigation.[13] (See model subpoena at Appendix A.)

2. Staff Depositions

Committees normally rely on informal staff interviews to gather information preparatory to investigations hearings. However, with more frequency in recent years, congressional committees have utilized staff-conducted depositions as a tool in exercising the investigatory power. Staff depositions afford a number of significant advantages for committees engaged in complex investigations. Staff depositions may assist committees in obtaining sworn testimony quickly and confidentially without the necessity of Members devoting time to lengthy hearings that may be unproductive because witnesses do not have the facts needed by the committee or refuse to cooperate. Depositions are conducted in private and may be more conducive to candid responses than would be the case at a public hearing. Statements made by witnesses that might defame or even tend to incriminate third parties can be verified before they are repeated in an open hearing. Depositions can prepare a committee for the questioning of witnesses at a hearing or provide a screening process that can obviate the need to call some witnesses. The deposition process also allows questioning of witnesses outside of

---

[9] *See, e.g.,* House Committee on Government Reform Rule 18(d); Senate Committee on Governmental Affairs Rule 5.C.

[10] U.S. Constitution, Art. I, see 6, cl.1.

[11] *Eastland v. United States Servicemen's Fund,* 421 U.S. 491, 503-07 (1975).

[12] 365 U.S. 399, 408-09 (1961).

[13] *In re Chapman,* 166 U.S. 661, 669 (1897).

Washington, thereby avoiding the inconvenience of conducting field hearings requiring the presence of Members.

Moreover, Congress has enhanced the efficacy of the staff deposition process by re-establishing the applicability of 18 U.S.C. 1001 to false statements made during congressional proceedings, including the taking of depositions.[14]

Certain disadvantages may also inhere. Unrestrained staff may be tempted to engage in tangential inquiries. Also, depositions present a "cold record" of a witness's testimony and may not be as useful for Members as in-person presentations.

At present, neither house of Congress has rules that expressly authorize staff depositions. On a number occasions such specific authority has been granted pursuant to Senate and House resolutions.[15] When granted, a committee will normally adopt procedures for taking depositions, including provisions for notice (with or without a subpoena), transcription of the deposition, the right to be accompanied by counsel, and the manner in which objections to questions are to be resolved.

3. Congressional Grants of Immunity

The Fifth Amendment to the Constitution provides in part that "no person... shall be compelled in any criminal case to be a witness against himself. . ."The privilege against self-incrimination is available to a witness in a congressional investigation.[16] When a witness before a committee asserts this testimonial constitutional privilege, the committee may, upon a two-thirds vote of the full committee, obtain a court order that compels and grants immunity against the use of testimony and information derived from that testimony in a subsequent criminal prosecution. The witness may still be prosecuted on the basis of other evidence. Grants of Immunity have figured prominently in a number of major congressional investigations, including Watergate (John Dean and Jeb Magruder) and Iran-Contra (Oliver North and John Poindexter). The decision to grant immunity involves a number of complex issues (see box below), but is ultimately a political decision that Congress makes. As observed by Iran-Contra Independent Counsel Lawrence E. Walsh, "The legislative branch has the power to decide whether it is more important perhaps even to destroy a prosecution than to hold back testimony they need. They make that decision. It is not a judicial decision or a legal decision but a political decision of the highest importance."[17]

---

[14] False Statements Accountability Act of 1996, Public Law 104-292. Congress acted in response to the Supreme Court's decision in *Hubbard v. United States,* 514 U.S. 695 (1995), holding that 18 U.S.C. 1001 applied only to false statements made in executive branch department and agency proceedings.

[15] See Jay R. Shampansky, Staff Depositions in Congressional Investigations, CRS Report No. 95-949, December 7, 1999, at notes 16 and 18.

[16] *Watkins v. United States,* 354 U.S. 178 (1957); *Quinn v. United States*, 349 U.S. 155 (1955).

[17] Lawrence E. Walsh, The Independent Counsel and the Separation of Powers, 25 House. L. rev. 1, 9 (1988).

Granting Immunity

In determining whether to grant immunity to a witness, a committee might wish to consider, on the one hand, its need for the witness's testimony in order to perform its legislative, oversight, and informing functions, and on the other, the possibility that the witness' immunized congressional testimony could jeopardize a successful criminal prosecution. If a witness is prosecuted after giving immunized testimony, the burden is on the prosecutor to establish that the case was not based on the witness's previous testimony or evidence derived there from. Kastigar v. United States, 406 U.S. 441, 460 (1972).

Appellate court decisions reversing the convictions of key Iran-Contra figures Lt. Colonel Oliver North and Rear Admiral John Poindexter appear to have made the prosecutorial burden substantially more difficult, if not insurmountable, in high-profile cases. Despite extraordinary efforts by the independent counsel and his staff to avoid being exposed to any of North's or Poindexter's immunized testimony, and the submission of sealed packets of evidence to the district court to show that the material was obtained independently of any immunized testimony to Congress, the appeals court in both cases remanded the cases for a further determination whether the prosecution had directly or indirectly used immunized testimony. Upon remand in both cases, the independent counsel moved to dismiss the prosecutions upon his determination that he could not meet the strict standards set by the appeals court in its decisions. See *United States* v. *North,* 910 F. 2d 843 (D.C. Cir.), *modified,* 920 F. 2d940 (D.C. Cir. 1990), *cert denied,* 500 U.S. 941 (1991); *United States v. Poindexter,* 951 F. 2d 369 (D.C. Cir. 1991). A consequence of the ruling was an increased reluctance, until the 105 Congress, on the part of committees to issue immunity grants.

C. ENFORCEMENT OF THE INVESTIGATIVE POWER

1. The Contempt Power

While the threat or actual issuance of a subpoena normally provides sufficient leverage to ensure compliance, it is through the contempt power, or its threat, that Congress may act with ultimate force in response to actions that obstruct the legislative process in order to punish the contemnor and/or to remove the obstruction. The Supreme Court early recognized the power as an inherent attribute of Congress's legislative authority, reasoning that if it did not possess this power, it "would be exposed to every indignity and interruption that rudeness, caprice or even conspiracy may mediate against it."[18]

There are three different kinds of contempt proceedings. Both the House and Senate may cite a witness for contempt under their inherent contempt power or under a statutory criminal contempt procedure. The Senate also has a third option, enforcement by means of a statutory civil contempt procedure.[19]

---

[18] *Anderson v. Dunn*, 19 U.S. (6 Wheat.) 204 (1821).
[19] For a more comprehensive treatment of the history and legal development of the congressional contempt power, see Jay R. Shampansky, Congress' Contempt Power, CRS Report No. 86-93A, February 28, 1986.

(a) Inherent Contempt

Under the inherent contempt power, the individual is brought before the House or Senate by the sergeant-at-arms, tried at the bar of the body, and can be imprisoned.

The purpose of the imprisonment or other sanction may be either punitive or coercive. Thus, the witness can be imprisoned for a specified period of time as punishment, or for an indefinite period (but not, at least in the case of the House, beyond the end of the Congress) until he agrees to comply. The inherent contempt power has not been exercised by either House in over 60 years because it has been considered to be too cumbersome and time consuming.

(b) Statutory Contempt

Recognizing the problems with use of the inherent contempt process, a statutory criminal contempt procedure was enacted in 1857 that, with only minor amendments, is codified today as 2 U.S.C. §§192 and 194. A person who has been subpoenaed to testify or produce documents before the House or Senate or a committee and who fails to do so, or who appears but refuses to respond to questions, is guilty of a misdemeanor, punishable by a fine of up to $100,000 and imprisonment for up to one year. A contempt citation must be approved by the subcommittee, the full committee, and the full House or Senate (or by the presiding officer if Congress is not in session). After a contempt has been certified by the President of the Senate or the Speaker of the House, it is the "duty" of the U.S. attorney "to bring the matter before the grand jury for its action."

(c) Civil Contempt

As an alternative to both the inherent contempt power of each house and criminal contempt, a civil contempt procedure is available in the Senate. Upon application of the Senate, the federal district court issues an order to a person refusing, or threatening to refuse, to comply with a Senate subpoena. If the individual still refuses to comply, he may be tried by the court in summary proceedings for contempt of court, with sanctions imposed to coerce compliance. Civil contempt can be more expeditious than a criminal proceeding, and it also provides an element of flexibility, allowing the subpoenaed party to test legal defenses in court without necessarily risking a criminal prosecution. Civil contempt is not authorized for use against executive branch officials refusing to comply with a subpoena except in certain limited circumstances.[20]

2. Perjury and False Statements Prosecutions
(a) Testimony Under Oath

A witness under oath before a congressional committee who willfully gives false testimony is subject to prosecution for perjury under section 1621 of title 18 of the United States Code. The false statement must be "willfully" made before a "competent tribunal" and involve a "material matter." For a legislative committee to be competent for perjury purposes

---

[20] 2 U.S.C. 288 d.

a quorum must be present.[21] The problem has been ameliorated in recent years with the adoption of rules establishing less than a majority of members as a quorum for taking testimony, normally two members for House committees[22] and one member for Senate committees.[23] The requisite quorum must be present at the time the alleged perjurious statement is made, not merely at the time the session convenes. No prosecution for perjury will lie for statements made only in the presence of committee staff unless the committee has deposition authority and has taken formal action to allow it.

(b) Unsworn Statements

Most statements made before Congress, at both the investigatory and hearing phases of oversight, are unsworn. The practice of swearing in all witnesses at hearings is infrequent. Prosecutions may be brought to punish congressional witnesses for giving willfully false testimony not under oath. Under 18 U.S.C. 1001, false statements by a person in "any investigation or review, conducted pursuant to the authority of any committee, subcommittee, commission or office of the Congress, consistent with applicable rules of the House and Senate" are punishable by a fine of up to $250,000 or imprisonment for not more than five years, or both.

D. EXECUTIVE PRIVILEGE AND COMMON LAW TESTIMONIAL PRIVILEGES

When Congress directs its investigatory powers at executive branch departments and agencies, and at times at the White House itself, such probes have often become contentious, provoking the executive to assert rights to shield from disclosure information Congress deems essential to carry out its oversight functions. The variety of grounds proffered are often lumped in an undifferentiated manner under the rubric "executive privilege." The courts recently have distinguished between claims of executive privilege based on whether it has been made by the President ("presidential communications privilege") or by a department or agency ("agency" or "executive privilege"). The distinction reflects the judicial recognition of the differing legal bases of the privileges (i.e., constitutional as opposed to common law) and the difference that makes in the evaluation of claims.

1. The Presidential Communications Privilege

In rare instances the executive response to a congressional demand to produce information may be an assertion of presidential executive privilege, a doctrine which, like Congress powers to investigate and cite for contempt, has constitutional roots. No decision of the Supreme Court has yet resolved the question whether there are any circumstances in

---

[21] *Christoffel v. United States*, 378 U.S. 89 (1949).
[22] House Rule XI (2)(h)(2).
[23] Senate Rule XXXVI(7)(a)(2) allows its committees to set a quorum requirement at less than the normal one-third for taking sworn testimony. Almost all Senate committees have set the quorum requirement at one member.

which the executive branch can refuse to provide information sought by the Congress on the basis of executive privilege. Indeed, most such disputes are settled short of litigation through employment of the political process and negotiations,[24] and the few that reach a judicial forum find the courts highly reluctant to rule on the merits. However, in *United States v. Nixon* (1974), involving a judicial subpoena issued to the President at the request of the Watergate special prosecutor,[25] the Supreme Court found a constitutional basis for the doctrine of executive privilege in "the supremacy of each branch within its own assigned area of constitutional duties" and in the separation of powers. Although it considered presidential communications to be "presumptively privileged," the Court rejected the President's contention that the privilege was absolute, precluding judicial review whenever it is asserted. The Court held in that case that the judicial need for the tapes outweighed the President's "generalized interest in confidentiality." The Court was careful to limit the scope of its decision, noting that "we are not here concerned with the balance between the President's generalized interest in confidentiality. . . and congressional demands for information."[26]

In *In re Sealed Case (Espy)*, involving a grand jury subpoena for documents to the White House Counsel's Office during an independent counsel's investigation of allegations of improprieties by the Secretary of Agriculture, an appeals court elaborated on several important issues left unresolved by *U.S. v. Nixon* and other Watergate-related cases: the precise parameters of the presidential executive privilege; how far down the chain of command the privilege reaches; whether the President has to have seen or had knowledge of the existence of the documents for which he claims privilege; and what showing is necessary to overcome a valid claim of privilege. The court held that the presidential communications privilege extended to communications authored by or solicited and received by presidential advisers that involved information regarding governmental operations that ultimately call for direct decision making by the President, but he does not have to actually have seen the documents for which he claims privilege, however, the privilege was held to be confined to White House staff, and not staff in agencies, and then only to White House staff that has "operational proximity" to direct presidential decision making. The claim of privilege may be overcome by a demonstration that each discrete group of subpoenaed materials likely contains important evidence, and that the evidence was not available with due diligence elsewhere, a showing which the court held the independent counsel had made.[27]

---

[24] Neal Devins, Congressional-Executive Information Access Disputes: A Modest Proposal: Do Nothing, Administrative Law Review, vol. 48, 109-137: Winter 1996; Joel D. Bush, Congressional-Executive Access Disputes: Legal Standards and Political Settlements, Journal of Law and Politics, vol. 9, 717:1993; Stephen W. Stathis, Executive Cooperation: Presidential Recognition of the Investigatory Authority of Congress and the Courts, Journal of Law and Politics, vol.3, 183:1986.

[25] The subpoena was for certain tape recordings and documents relating to the President's conversations with aides and advisors. The materials were sought for use in a criminal trial.

[26] 418 U.S. 683, 712n. 19(1974). In *Senate Select Committee on Presidential Campaign Activities* v. *Nixon,* 498 F. 2d 725 (D.C. Cir. 1974), decided prior to *U.S.* v. *Nixon,* the appeals court denied the Watergate Committee's access to five presidential tapes because the committee had not met its burden of showing that "the subpoenaed evidence is demonstrably critical to the responsible fulfillment of the Committee's function." The court noted that its denial was based upon the initiation of impeachment proceedings by the House Judiciary Committee, the overlap of the investigative objectives of both committees, and the fact that the impeachment committee already had the tapes in question, concluding that "The Select Committee's immediate oversight need for the subpoenaed tapes is, from a congressional perspective, merely cumulative." The unique and confining nature of the case's factual and historical context likely makes this an uncertain precedent for limiting a committee's investigatory power in the face of a presidential claim of privilege.

[27] 121 F.3d 729 (D.C. Cir. 1997).

Since the Kennedy Administration, executive policy directives establish that presidential executive privilege maybe asserted only by the President personally. The latest such directive, issued by President Reagan in November 1982, and still in effect, requires that when agency heads believe that a congressional information request raises substantial questions of executive privilege they are to notify and consult with the attorney general and the counsel to the President. If the matter is deemed to justify invocation of the privilege, it is reported to the President who makes his decision (See Reagan memo at Appendix B).

However, a memorandum of September 28, 1994, from White House Counsel Lloyd Cutler to all department and agency general counsels modified the Reagan policy by requiring agency heads directly to notify the White House Counsel of any congressional request for "any document created in the White House . . . or in a department or agency, that contains deliberations of, or advice to or from, the White house" that may raise privilege issues. The White House counsel is to seek an accommodation and, if that does not succeed, he is to consult the attorney general to determine whether to recommend invocation of privilege to the President. The President then determines whether to claim privilege, which is then communicated to the Congress by the White House Counsel. Thus, it would appear that decision making with respect to claims of presidential privilege is now fully centralized in the White House, but that the President must still personally assert the claim. (See Cutler memo at Appendix C). The current Bush Administration has as yet taken no public position on the Reagan memorandum or the Cutler modification.

2. Common-Law Testimonial Privileges

More common are claims by departments and agencies (and at times by the White House), and by private persons, that common law testimonial privileges, such as the attorney-client, work-product, and deliberative-process privileges, afford a shield to congressional investigative inquiries. Although there has never been a definitive Supreme Court ruling on the question, the strong constitutional underpinnings of the legislative investigatory power, long-standing congressional practice, and recent appellate court rulings casting doubt on the viability of common-law privilege claims by executive officials in the face of grand jury investigations, support the position that committees may determine, on a case-by case basis, whether to accept a claim of privilege.

Thus it is well established by congressional practice that acceptance of a claim of attorney-client, work product or other common law testimonial privilege before a committee rests in the sound discretion of that committee. Such common-law privileges cannot be claimed as a matter of right by a witness, and a committee can branch officials may claim attorney-client, work product or deliberative process privileges in the face of investigative demands of a grand jury.[28] In actual practice, all committees that have denied claims of privilege have engaged in a process of weighing considerations of legislative need, public policy, and the statutory duties of congressional committees to engage in continuous oversight of the application, administration, and execution of the laws that fall within its

---

[28] Glenn A. Beard, Congress v. The Attorney-Client Privilege: A "Full and Frank" Discussion, American Criminal Law Review, Vol. 35, 119: 1997; Morton Rosenberg, Investigative Oversight: An Introduction to the Law,

jurisdiction, against any possible injury to the witness. Committees, among other factors, have considered whether a court would have recognized the claim in the judicial forum.[29] Moreover, the conclusion that recognition of nonconstitutionally based privileges is a matter of congressional discretion is consistent with both traditional British parliamentary and the Congress's historical practice.[30]

The legal basis for Congress's prerogative in this area is based upon its inherent constitutional prerogative to investigate, which has been long recognized by the Supreme Court as extremely broad and encompassing, and which is at its peak when the subject is fraud, abuse, or maladministration within a government department.[31] Common-law privileges are, on the other hand, judge-made exceptions to the normal principle of full disclosure in the adversary process, which is to be narrowly construed and has been confined to the judicial forum. These privileges have no constitutional basis.[32] Recent appellate court rulings have cast substantial doubt whether executive branch officials may claim attorney-client, work product or deliberative process privileges in the face of investigative demands of a grand jury.[33]

While no court has as yet recognized the inapplicability of common law testimonial privileges in congressional proceedings,[34] in a decision directly addressing the issue,[35] an

---

Practice and Procedure of Congressional Inquiry," CRS Report No. 95-46A, 43-56 (April 7, 1995) (CRS Report).

[29] See, *e.g.*, "Contempt of Congress Against Franklin L. Haney," H. Rept. No. 105-792, 105th Cong., 2d Sess. 11-16 (1988); "Proceedings Against John M. Quinn, David Watkins, and Matthew Moore (Pursuant to Title 2, United States Code, Sections 192 and 194)," H.Rept.No. 104-598, 104th Cong. 2d Sess. 50-54 (1996); "Refusal of William H. Kennedy, III, To Produce Notes Subpoenaed By The Special Committee to Investigate Whitewater Development Corporation and Related Matters," Sen. Rept., No. 104-191, 104th Cong. 1st Sess. 9-19 (1995); "Proceedings Against Ralph Bernstein and Joseph Bernstein," H.Rept. No. 99-462, 99th Cong. 2d Sess. 13, 14 (1986); Hearings, "International Uranium Control," Before the Subcommittee on Oversight and Investigations, House Committee on Interstate and Foreign Commerce, 95th Cong. 1st Sess. 60, 123 (1977).

[30] See, CRS Report, *supra* note 28, at 44-49.

[31] *McGrain v. Daugherty*, 272 U.S. 135, 177 (1926); *Watkins v. United States*, 354 U.S. 178, 187 (1957); *Eastland v. United States Servicemen's Fund*, 421 U.S. 491, 504 n. 15 (1975).

[32] *Westinghouse Electric Corp. v. Republic of the Philippines*, 951 F.2d 1414, 1423 (3d Cir. 1991) ("Because the attorney-client privilege obstructs the truth-finding process, it is narrowly construed." *Moran v. Burbine* 475 U.S. 412, 430 (1986) (Sixth Amendment not a source for attorney-client privilege); *Fisher v. United States*, 425 U.S. 391, 396-97 (1976) (compelling on attorney to disclose client communications does not violate the client's Fifth Amendment privilege against self-incrimination); *Hannah v. Larche*, 363 U.S. 420, 425 (1960) ("Only infrequently have witnesses [in congressional hearings] been afforded rights normally associated with an adjudicative proceeding"); *United States v. Fort*, 443 U.S. 932 (1971) (rejecting contention that the constitutional right to cross-examine witnesses applied to congressional investigations); *In re Sealed Case (Espy)*, 121 F.3d 729 (D.C. Cir. 1997) (the deliberative process privilege is a common law privilege which, when claimed by executive officials, is easily overcome, and "disappears" altogether upon the reasonable belief by an investigating body that government misconduct has occurred).

[33] *In re Grand Jury Subpoena Duces Tecum*, 112 F.3d 910 (8th Cir. 1997), *cert. Denied sub. Nom. Office of the President v. Office of the Independent Counsel*, 521 U.S. 1105 (1997)(claims of First Lady of attorney-client and work-product privilege with respect notes taken by White House Counsel Office attorneys rejected); *IN re Bruce R. Lindsey (Grand Jury Testimony)*, 158 F.3d 1263 (D.C. Cir. 1998), *cert. Denied* 525 U.S. 996 (1998) (White House attorney may not invoke attorney-client privilege in response to grand jury subpoena seeking information on possible commission of federal crimes); *In re Sealed Case (Espy)*, 121 F.3d 729 (D.C. Cir. 1997) (deliberative process privilege is a common law agency privilege which easily overcome by showing of need by an investigating body).

[34] Opinion No. 288, "Compliance With Subpoena from Congressional Committee to Produce Lawyers' Files Containing Client Confidences or Secrets," Legal Ethics Committee, District of Columbia Bar, February 16, 1999. (D.C. Ethics Committee Opinion).

[35] The Supreme Court has recognized that "only infrequently have witnesses... [in congressional hearings] been afforded the procedural rights normally associated with an adjudicative proceedings." *Hannah v. Larche*, 363 US. 420, 425 (1960); see also, *United States v. Fort*, 443 F.2d 670 (D.C. Cir. 1970), *cert denied*, 403 U.S. 932

opinion issued by Legal Ethics Committee of the District of Columbia Bar in February 1999, provides substantial support for the longstanding congressional practice. The occasion for the ruling arose as a result of an investigation of a Subcommittee of the House Committee into the circumstances surrounding the planned relocation of the Federal Communications Commission to the Portals office complex.[36] During the course of the inquiry, the Subcommittee sought certain documents from the Portals developer, Mr. Franklin L. Haney. Mr. Haney's refusal to comply resulted in subpoenas for those documents to him and the law firm representing him during the relocation efforts. Haney and the law firm asserted attorney-client privilege in their continued refusal to comply. The law firm sought an opinion from D.C. Bar's Ethics Committee as to its obligations in the face of the subpoena and a possible contempt citation, but the Bar Committee notified the firm that the question was novel and that no advice could be given until the matter was considered in a plenary session of the Committee.[37] The firm continued its refusal to comply until the Subcommittee cited it for contempt, at which time the firm proposed to turn over the documents if the contempt citation was withdrawn. The Subcommittee agreed to the proposal.[38]

Subsequently, on February 16, 1999, the D.C. Bar's Ethics Committee issued an opinion vindicating the action taken by the firm. The Ethics Committee, interpreting D.C. Rule of Professional Conduct 1.6(d)(2)(A),[39] held that an attorney faced with a congressional subpoena that would reveal client confidences or secrets

> Has a professional responsibility to seek to quash or limit the subpoena on all available, legitimate grounds to protect confidential documents and client secrets. If, thereafter, the Congressional subcommittee overrules these objections, orders production of the documents and threatens to hold the lawyer in contempt absent compliance with the subpoena, then, in the absence of a judicial order forbidding the production, the lawyer is permitted, but not required, by the D.C. Rules of Professional Conduct to produce the subpoenaed documents. A directive of a Congressional subcommittee accompanied by a threat of fines and imprisonment pursuant to federal criminal law satisfies the standard of "required by law" as that phrase is used in D.C. Rule of Professional conduct 1.6(d)(2)(A).

The D.C. Bar opinion urges attorneys to press every appropriate objection to the subpoena until no further avenues of appeal are available, and even suggests that clients might be advised to retain other counsel to institute a third-party action to enjoin compliance,[40] arouse

---

(1971) (rejecting the contention that the constitutional right to cross-examine witnesses applied to a congressional investigation); *IN the Matter of Provident Life and Accident Co.,* E.D. Tenn., S.D. CIV-1-90-219, June 13, 1990 (per Edgar, J.)(Noting that the court's earlier ruling on an attorney-client privilege claim was "not of constitutional dimensions, and is certainly not binding on the Congress of the United States".).

[36] See, H.Report No. 105-792, *supra* note 29, at 1-6, 7-8, 15-16.

[37] See, "Meeting on Portals Investigation (Authorization of Subpoenas; Receipt of Subpoenaed Documents and Consideration of Objections; and Contempt of Congress Proceedings Against Franklin L. Haney)," H. Comm. On Commerce, 105th Cong., 2d Sess. 48-50 (1998).

[38] *Id.,* at 101-105.

[39] Under Rule 1.6(d)(2)(A) a lawyer may reveal client confidences or secrets only when expressly permitted by the D.C. rules or when "required by law or court order."

[40] A direct suit to enjoin a committee from enforcing a subpoena has been foreclosed by the Supreme Court's decision in *Eastland v. United States Servicemen's Fund,* 421 U.S. 491, 501 (10975), but that ruling does not appear to foreclose an action against a "third party," such as the client's attorney, to test the validity of the subpoena or the power of a committee to refuse to recognize the privilege. See, *e.g., United States v. AT&T,* 567 F.2d 121 (D.C. Cir. 1977) (entertaining an action by the Justice Department to enjoin AT&T 567 F.2d

a controversial and sensitive debate,[41] particularly if congressional committees choose to subpoena client documents from attorneys as a matter of course.

Assertions of deliberative process privilege by agencies have not been uncommon in the past. In essence it is argued that congressional demands for information as to what occurred during the policy development process of an agency would unduly interfere, and perhaps "chill," the frank and open internal communications necessary to the quality and integrity of the decisional process. It may also be grounded on the contentions that it protects against premature disclosure of proposed policies before they are fully considered or actually adopted by the agency, and to prevent the public from confusing matters merely considered or discussed during the deliberative process with those on which the decision was based. However, as with claims of attorney-client privilege and work produce immunity discussed previously, congressional practice has been to treat their acceptance as discretionary with the committee. Moreover, a recent appellate court decision underlines the understanding that the deliberative process privilege is a common law privilege of agencies that it easily overcome by a showing of need by an investigatory body, and other court rulings and congressional practice have recognized the overriding necessity of an effective legislative oversight process.

The recent appeals court ruling in *In re sealed Case (Espy)*[42] is of special note. The case involved, *inter alia*, White House claims of executive and deliberate process privileges for documents subpoenaed by an independent counsel. At the outset of the appeals court's unanimous ruling it carefully distinguished between the "presidential communications privilege" and the "deliberative process privilege." Both, the court observed, are executive privileges designed to protect the confidentiality of executive branch decisionmaking. But the deliberative process privilege applies to executive branch officials generally, is a common law privilege which requires a lower threshold of need to be overcome, and "disappears altogether when there is any reason to believe government misconduct has occurred."[43] The court's recognition of the deliberative process privilege as a common law privilege which, when claimed by executive department and agency officials, is easily overcome, and which "disappears" upon the reasonable belief by an investigating body that government misconduct has occurred, may severely limit the common law claims of agencies against congressional investigative demands. A demonstration of need of a jurisdictional committee would appear to be sufficient, and a plausible showing of fraud waste, abuse or maladministration would be conclusive.

---

121 (D.C. Cir. 1977) (entertaining an action by the Justice Department to enjoin AT&T from complying with a subpoena to provide telephone records that might compromise national security matters).

[41] See, *e.g.,* W.John Moore, "First Save All The Lawyers," National Law Journal, July 24, 1999 at 2170.

[42] 121 F. 3d 729 (C.D. Cir. 1997).

[43] 121 F.3d at 745, 746; see also *id.* At 737-738 ("[W]here there is reason to believe the documents sought may shed light on government misconduct, the [deliberative process] privilege is routinely denied on the grounds that shielding internal government deliberations in this context does not serve 'the public interest in honest, effective government").

E. INVESTIGATIVE OVERSIGHT HEARINGS

1. Jurisdiction and Authority

A congressional committee is a creation of its parent house and only has the power to inquire into matters within the scope of the authority that has been delegated to it by that body. Thus, the enabling rule or resolution which gives the committee life is the charter that defines the grant and limitations of the committee's power. In construing the scope of a committee's authorizing charter, courts will look to the words of the rule or resolution itself, and then, if necessary, to the usual sources of legislative history such as floor debate, legislative reports, past committee practice, and interpretation. Jurisdiction authority for "special" investigations may be given to a standing committee, a joint committee of both houses, or a special subcommittee of a standing committee, among other vehicles. In view of the specificity with which Senate and House rules now confer jurisdiction on standing committee, as well as the care with which most authorizing resolutions for select committees have been drafted in recent years, sufficient models exist to avoid a successful judicial challenge by a witness that his noncompliance was justified by a committee's overstepping its delegated scope of authority.

2. Rules Applicable to Hearings

House Rule XI(2) and Senate Rule XXVI(2) require that committees adopt written rules of procedure and publish them in the *Congressional Record*. The failure to publish has resulted in the invalidation of a perjury prosecution.[44] Once properly promulgated, such rules are judicially cognizable and must be strictly observed. The House and many individual Senate committees require that all witnesses by given a copy of a committee's rules.

Both the House and the Senate have adopted rules permitting a reduced quorum for taking testimony and receiving evidence. House hearings may be conducted if at least two members are present; most Senate committees permit hearings with only one member in attendance. Although most committees have adopted the minimum quorum requirement, some have not, while others require a higher quorum for sworn rather than unsworn testimony. For perjury purposes, the quorum requirement must be met at the time the allegedly perjured testimony is given, not at the beginning of the session. Reduced quorum requirement rules do not apply to authorizations for the issuance of subpoenas. Senate rules require a one-third quorum of a committee or subcommittee while the House requires a quorum of a majority of the members, unless a committee delegates authority for issuance to its chairman.[45]

Senate and House rules limit the authority of their committees to meet in closed session. A House rule provides that testimony "shall" be held in closed session if a majority of a committee or subcommittee determines it "may tend to defame, degrade, or incriminate any person." Such testimony taken in closed session is normally releasable only by a majority

---

[44] *United States v. Reinecke*, 524 F.2d 435 (D.C. Cir. 1975)(failure to publish committee rule setting one Senator as a quorum for taking hearing testimony held a sufficient ground to reverse a perjury conviction).

[45] Senate Rule XXVI(7)(a)(1); House Rule XI(2)(m)(3).

vote of the committee. Similarly, confidential material received in a closed session requires a majority vote for release.

3. Conducting Hearings

The chair usually makes an opening statement. In the case of an investigative hearing, it is an important means of defining the subject matter of the hearing and thereby establishing the pertinence of questions asked the witnesses. Not all committees swear in their witnesses; a few committees require that all witnesses by sworn. Most committees leave the swearing of witnesses to the discretion of the chair. If a committee wishes the potential sanction of perjury to apply, it should swear its witnesses, though false statements not under oath are subject to criminal sanctions.

A witness does not have a right to make a statement before being questioned but that opportunity is usually accorded. Committee rules may prescribe the length of such statements and also require written statements be submitted in advance of the hearing. Questioning of witnesses may be structured so that members alternate for specified lengths of time. Questioning may also be conducted by staff. Witnesses may be allowed to review a transcript of their testimony and to make nonsubstantive corrections.

The right of a witness to be accompanied by counsel is recognized by House rule and the rules of Senate committees. The House rule limits the role of counsel as solely "for the purpose of advising them concerning their constitutional rights." Some committees have adopted rules specifically prohibiting counsel from "coaching" witnesses during their testimony.[46] A committee has complete authority to control the conduct of counsel. Indeed, House Rule XI(2)(k)(4) provides that "[t]he chairman may punish breaches of order and decorum, and of professional ethics on the part of counsel, by censure or exclusion from the hearings; and the Committee may cite the offender for contempt." Some Senate committees have adopted similar rules.[47] There is no right of cross-examination of adverse witnesses during an investigative hearing. Witnesses are entitled to a range of constitutional protections (see box).

---

[46] See, *e.g.*, Senate Permanent Committee on Investigations Rule 8.
[47] See, *e.g.*, Senate Aging Committee Rule V.8; Senate Permanent Subcommittee on Investigations Rule 7.

Constitutional Rights of Witnesses

It is well established that the protections of the Bill of Rights extend to witnesses at legislative inquiry and thus may pose significant limitations on congressional investigations. The Fifth Amendment provides that "no person ... shall be compelled in any criminal case to be a witness against himself." The privilege protects a witness against being compelled to testify subject to a grant of immunity (see pages 35 and 36) but not against a subpoena for existing documentary evidence. However, where compliance with a subpoena *duces tecum* would constitute an implicit testimonial authentication of the documents produced, the privilege may apply. There is no particular formulation of words necessary to invoke the privilege. All that is required is that the whiteness's objection be stated in a manner that the committee may reasonably expected to understand as an attempt to invoke the privilege.

Although the First Amendment, by its terms, is expressly applicable only to *legislation* that abridges freedom of speech, press, or assembly, the Court has held that the amendment also restricts Congress in conducting investigations. In the leading case involved the application of First Amendment rights in a congressional investigation, *Barenblatt v. United States*, the Court held that "where first amendment rights are asserted to bar government interrogation resolution of the issue always involves a balancing by the courts of the competing private and public interests at stake in the particular circumstances shown." 360 U.S. 109, 162 (1959). Thus, unlike the Fifth Amendment privilege against self-incrimination, the First Amendment does not give a witness an absolute right to respond to congressional demands for information.

Dicta in opinions of the Supreme Court indicate that the Fourth Amendment's prohibition against unreasonable searches and seizures is applicable to congressional committees. It appears that there must be probable cause for the issuance of a congressional subpoena. The Fourth Amendment protects a congressional witness against a subpoena that is unreasonably broad or burdensome.

F. SPECIALIZED INVESTIGATIONS

Oversight at times occurs through specialized, temporary investigations of a specific event or development. These are often dramatic, high profile endeavors, focusing on scandals, alleged abuses of authority, suspected illegal conduct, or other unethical behavior. The stakes are high, possibly even leading to the end of individual careers of high ranking executive officials. Indeed, congressional investigations can induce resignations, firings, and impeachment proceedings, as the Senate Watergate committee investigation did in the Nixon Administration and as occurred as a result of the multiple investigations during the Clinton Administration. As a consequence, interest – in Congress, the executive, and the public – is frequently intense and impassioned.

Prominent Select Investigative Committees

Senate Watergate committee (1973-74). S. Res. 60, 93d Congress, 1st Session.

"To establish a select committee of the Senate to conduct an investigation and study of the extent, if any, to which illegal, improper, or unethical activities were engaged in by any persons, acting individually or in combination with others, in the presidential election of 1972, or any campaign, canvass, or other activity related to it."

House Select Committee on the Iran-Contra Affair (1987). H. Res. 12, 100th Congress, 1st Session.

"The select committee is authorized and directed to conduct a full and complete investigation and study, and to make such findings and recommendations to the House as the select committee deems appropriate," regarding the sale or transfer of arms, technology, or intelligence to Iran or Iraq; the diversion of funds realized in connection with such sales and otherwise, to the anti-government forces in Nicaragua; the violation of any law, agreement, promise, or understanding regarding the reporting to and informing of Congress; operational activities and the conduct of foreign and national security policy by the staff of the National Security Council; authorization and supervision or lack thereof of such matters by the President and other White house personnel; the role of individuals and entities outside.

1. These investigative hearings may be *televised* in the contemporary era, and often result in *extensive news media coverage*.

2. Such investigations may be undertaken by *different organizational arrangements*. These include temporary select committees, standing committees and their subcommittees, specially created subcommittees, or specially commissioned task forces within an existing standing committee.

3. Specially created investigative committees usually have a *short life span: e.g.,* six months, one year, or at the longest until the end of a Congress, at which point the panel would have to be reapproved if the inquiry were to continue.

4. The investigative panel often has to *employ additional and special staff* – including investigators, attorneys, auditors, and researchers – because of the added work load and need for specialized expertise in conducting such investigations and in the subject matter. Such staff can be hired under contract from the private sector, transferred from existing congressional offices or committees, transferred from the congressional support agencies, or loaned by executive agencies, including the Federal Bureau of Investigation. The staff would require appropriate security clearances if the inquiry looked into matters of national security.

5. Such special panels have often been vested with investigative authorities not ordinarily available to standing committees. Staff deposition authority is the most commonly given, but given the particular circumstances, special panels have been vested with the authority to obtain tax information, to seek international assistance in information gathering efforts abroad, and to participate in judicial proceedings (see chart).

Table 1. Special Investigative Authorities of Selected Investigating Committees[1]

	Deposition Authority	International Information Gathering Authority	Tax Information Access Authority	Authority to Participate in Judicial Proceedings
Sen. Select Committee on Watergate[2]	Member/Staff	No	No	Yes
Nixon Impeachment Proceedings[3]	Member/Staff	Yes	No	No
House Assassinations Inquiry[4]	Member/Staff	Yes	No	No
Church Committee[5]	Member/Staff	Yes	No	No
Koreagate[6]	Member/Staff	Yes	No	No
ABSCAM (House)[7]	Member	Letters Rogatory	No	Yes, by special counsel
Iran-Contra House[9]	Member/Staff	Letters Rogatory, Commissions, Depositions	Yes	Yes
Judge Hastings Impeachment[11]	Staff	No	No	No
Judge Nixon Impeachment[12]	Staff	No	No	No
October Surprise[13]	Staff	Letters Rogatory, Commissions, Depositions	Yes	Yes
Senate Whitewater (II)[14]	Staff	Letters Rogatory, Commissions	Yes	No
White House Travel office[15]	Member/Staff	No	No	No
House Campaign Finance[16]	Member/Staff	Letters Rogatory, Commissions	Yes	Yes, by House General Counsel
Select Committee on National Security Commercial Concerns[17]	Member/Staff	Letters Rogatory, Depositions	Yes	Yes, by House General Counsel
Teamsters Election Investigation[18]	Member/Staff	No	No	No

1   More comprehensive compilations of authorities and rules of Senate and House special investigatory committees may be found in Senate Committee on Rules and Administration, "Authority and Rules of Senate Special Investigatory Committees and Other Senate Entities, 1973-97," Sen. Doc. 105-16, 105th Cong. 1st Sess. (1998), and Jay Shampansky, "Staff Depositions in Congressional Investigations," CRS Report 95-949 (Updated December 3, 1999), at notes 16 and 18.

2   S.Res. 60 and Sen. Res. 194, 93rd Congress, 1973.

3   H. Res. 803, 93rd Congress, 1974.

4   H. Res. 222, 95th Congress, 1974.

5   S. Res. 21, 94th Congress, 1974.

6   H.Res. 252, and H.Res. 752, 95th Congress, 1977.

7   H. Res. 67, 97th Congress, 1981.

8   S. Res. 350, 97th Congress, 1982.

9   H. Res. 12, 10th Congress, 1987.

10   S. Res. 23, 100th Congress, 1987.

11   H. Res. 320, 100th Congress, 1987.

12   H. Res.562, 100th Congress, 1988.

13   H. Res. 258, 102d Congress, 1991.

14   S. Res. 120, 104th Congress, 1995.

15   H. Res. 369, 104th Congress, 1996.

16   H. Res. 167, 105th Congress, 1997.

17   H. Res. 463, 105th Congress, 1998.

18   H. Res. 507, 105th Congress, 1998.

G. ROLE OF MINORITY-PARTY MEMBERS
IN THE INVESTIGATIVE PROCESS

The role of members of the minority in the investigatory oversight process is governed by the rules of each house and its committees. While minority members are specifically accorded some rights (*e.g.*, in the House of Representatives, whenever a hearing is conducted on any measure or matter, the minority m ay, upon the written request of a majority of the minority members to the chairman before the completion of the hearing, call witnesses selected by the minority, and presumably request documents[48], no House or committee rules authorize either ranking minority members or individual members on their own to institute official committee investigations, hold hearings, or issue subpoenas.   Individual members may seek the voluntary cooperation of agency officials or private persons. But no judicial precedent has directly recognized a right in an individual member, other than the chair of a committee,[49] to exercise the authority of a committee in the context of oversight without the permission of a majority of the committee or its chair.   Moreover, a 1994 federal district court ruling dismissed the attempt of the then-ranking minority member of the House Banking [now titled Financial Services] Committee to compel disclosure of documents from two agencies under the Freedom of Information Act and the Administrative Procedure Act. The court held that the case was one "in which a congressional plaintiff's dispute is primarily with his or her fellow legislators" and that the ranking minority member's "complaint derives solely from his failure to persuade his colleagues to authorize his request for the documents in question, and that Plaintiff thus has a clear 'collegial remedy' capable of affording him substantial relief."[50]

That court also suggested that the possibility that a "collegial remedy" for the minority exists already, pointing to 5 U.S.C. 2954, under which small groups of members of the House Government Reform and Senate Governmental Affairs Committees can request information from executive agencies without the need of formal committee action.[51] However, the precise scope and efficacy of this provision is uncertain.

5 U.S.C. 2954 is derived from section 2 of the Act of May 29, 1928,[52] which originally referred not to the current committees generally overseeing government agency operations but their predecessors, the House and Senate Committees on Expenditures in the Executive Departments.   The principal purpose of the 1928 act, embodied in its first section, was to repeal legislation that required the submission to the Congress of some 128 reports, many of

---

[48] House Rule XI2(j)(1); House Banking Committee Rule IV. 4.

[49] *Ashland Oil Co., Inc. v. FTC*, 548 F.2d 977, 979-80 (D.C. Cir. 1976), affirming 409 F.Supp. 297 (D.D.C. 1976). Se also *Exxon v. Federal Trade Commission*, 589 F.2d 582, 592-93 (D.C. Cir. 1978) (acknowledging that the "principle is important that disclosure of information can only be compelled by members …"); and *In re Beef Industry Antitrust Litigation*, 589 F.2d 786, 791 (5th Cir. 1979)(refusing to permit two congressmen from intervening in private litigation because they "failed to obtain a House Resolution or any similar authority before they sought to intervene.")

[50] *Leach v. Resolution Trust Corporation*, 860 F.Supp. 868, 874-76 (D.D.C. 1994).

[51] *Id.* At 876 note 7. 5 U.S.C. 2954 provides: "An Executive agency, on request of the Committee on Government [Reform] of the House of Representatives, or of any seven members thereof, or on request of the Committee on Government Operations of the senate, or any five members thereof, shall submit any information requested of it relating to any matter within the jurisdiction of the committee."

[52] 45 Stat. 996.

which had become obsolete in part, and which, in any event, had no value, served no useful purpose, and were not printed by the House of Representatives.[53]

Section 2 of the 1928 act contains the language that has between codified in 5 U.S.C. 2954. The legislative history, however, indicates that the purpose of the 1928 act was not to assert a sweeping right of Congress to obtain any information it might desire from the executive branch. Rather, the aim of the section appeared far more limited. Thus, the Senate report stated that its purpose was to make "it possible to require any report discontinued by the language of this bill to be resubmitted to either House upon its necessity becoming evident to the membership of either body."[54] Or, of Representatives to have furnished any of the information contained in the reports proposed to be abolished, a provision has been added to the bill requiring such information to be furnished to the Committee on Expenditures in the Executive Departments or upon the requires of any seven members thereof."[55]

It would appear, then, that the scope of 5 U.S.C. 2954 is closely tied to the 128 reports abolished by section 1 of the 1928 legislation.[56] Moreover, the provision lacks a compulsory component. Agency refusals to comply would not be subject to existing contempt processes, and the outcome of a civil suit to compel production on the basis of the provision is problematic despite the *Leach* court's suggestion. Further, the provision applies only to the named committees; thus members of all other committees would still face the *Leach* problem. Finally, even members of the named committees are still likely to have to persuade a court that their claim is more than an intramural dispute. The first attempt to secure court enforcement of a document demand under Section 2954 is currently pending in a federal district court.[57] The case involves a request of the minority party members of the House Government Reform Committee for information from the Secretary of Commerce for data concerning the 2000 census.

The rules of the Senate provide substantially more effective means for individual minority-party members to engage in "self-help" to support oversight objectives than afforded their House counterparts. Senate rules emphasize the rights and prerogatives of individual Senators and, therefore, minority groups of Senators.[58] The most important of these rules are those that effectively allow unlimited debate on a bill or amendment unless an extraordinary majority votes to invoke cloture.[59] Senators can use their right to filibuster, or simply the threat of filibuster, to delay or prevent the Senate from engaging in legislative business. The Senate's rules also are a source of other minority rights that can directly or indirectly aid the minority in gaining investigatory rights. For example, the right of extended debate applies in committee as well as on the floor, with one crucial difference: the Senate's cloture rule may not be invoked in committee. Each Senate committee decides for itself how it will control debate, and therefore a filibuster opportunity in a committee may be even greater than on the

---

[53] H.R. Rep. No. 1757, 70th Cong. 1st Sess., pp. 2-3 (1928). A study of the Bureau of Efficiency had recommended their elimination. H.R. Rep. 1757, at p. 2; S. Rep. No. 1320, 70th Cong., 1st Sess., p. 1 (1928).

[54] S. Rep. No. 1320, *supra.* At 4.

[55] H.R. Rep No. 1757, *supra,* at 1. This intent is supported by the House and Senate floor debates. See 69 Cong. Rec. 9413-17, 10613-16 (1928).

[56] In codifying Title 5 in 1966, Congress made it clear that it was effecting no substantive changes in existing laws: "The legislative purpose in enacting sections 1-6 of this Act is to restate, without substantive change, the laws replaced by those sections on the effective date of this Act." Pub. L. 898-544, sec. 7(a).

[57] *Waxman, et al. v. Evans,* Civ. Action No. 01-14530-LGB (AJWx) (D.C. CD Calif.)

[58] See Stanley Bach, Minority Rights and Senate Procedures, Congressional Research Service Report No. RL 30850, January 31, 2001.

[59] Senate Rules XIX and XXII.

floor. Also, Senate Rule XXVI prohibits the reporting of any measure or matter from a committee unless a majority of the committee is present, another point of possible tactical leverage. Even beyond the potent power to delay, Senators can promote their goals by taking advantage of other parliamentary rights and opportunities that are provided by the Senate's formal procedures and customary practices, such as are afforded by the processes dealing with floor recognition, committee referrals, and the amending process.[60]

SELECTED READINGS

Beard, Glenn A. Congress v. The Attorney-Client Privilege: A "Full and Frank" Discussion, American Criminal Law Review, v. 35, 1997: v. 35, 1997: 199.

Berger, Raoul. Congressional Subpoenas to Executive Officials. Columbia Law Review, v. 75, 1975: 865.

Berger, Raoul. Executive Privilege: A Constitutional Myth. Cambridge: Harvard University Press, 1974.

Brand. Stanley M. Battle Among the Branches: The Two Hundred Year War. North Carolina Law Review, v. 65, 1987: 901.

Brand, Stanley M. and Connelly, Sean. Constitutional Confrontations: Preserving a Prompt and Orderly Means by Which Congress May Enforce Investigative Demands Against Executive Branch Officials. Catholic University Law Review, v. 36, 1986: 71.
Bush, Joel D. Congressional Executive Access Disputes: Legal Standards and Political Settlements. Journal of Law and Politics, v. 9, Summer 1993: 719.

Claveleaux, Ronald L. The Conflict between Executive Privilege and Congressional Oversight: The Gorsuch Controversy. Duke Law Journal, v. 1983, No. 6: 1333.

Devins, Neal. Congressional-Executive Information Disputes: A Modest Proposal-Do Nothing. Administrative Law Review, vol. 48, Winter 1996: 109.

Dimock, Marshall E. Congressional Investigating Committees. Baltimore: Johns Hopkins University Press, 1929.

                                                                    JK 1123.A2E2

Fisher, Louis. Congressional Access to Executive Branch Information: Legislative Tools CRS Report No. RL 30966. May 17, 2001.

Ghio, R.S. The Iran-Contra Prosecutions and the Failure of Use Immunity. Stanford Law Review, v. 45, 1992: 229.

---

[60] See Bach, *supra* note 58 at pp. 8-11.

Grabow, John C. Congressional Investigations: Law and Practice. New Jersey: Prentice Hall Law and Business, 1988.

KF4942.H34

Hamilton, James. The Power to Probe: A Study in Congressional Investigations. New York: Vintage Books, 1976

KF4942.H34

Hamilton, James and Grabow John C. A Legislative Proposal for Resolving Executive Privilege Disputes Precipitated by Congressional Subpoenas. Harvard Journal Legislation, v. 21, Winter 1984: 145.

Moreland, Allen B. Congressional Investigations and Private Persons. Southern California Law Review, v. 40, Winter 1967: 189.

Peterson, Todd D. Prosecuting Executive Branch Officials For Contempt Of Congress. New York University Law Review, v. 66, 1991: 563.

Rosenberg, Morton. Investigative Oversight: An Introduction to the Law, Practice and Procedure of Congressional Inquiry. CRS Report No. 95-464A, April 7, 1995.

_____. Presidential Claims of Executive Privilege: History, Law, Practice and Recent Developments. CRS Report No. RL 30319, September 21, 1999.

Rosenthal, Paul C. and Grossman, Robert S. Congressional Access to Confidential Information Colleged by federal Agencies. Harvard Journal of Legislation, v. 15, 1977: 74.
Rozell, Mark J. Executive Privilege: The Dilemma of Secrecy and Democratic Accountability. Baltimore and London: The Johns Hopkins University Press, 1994.

Schlesinger, Arthur M. Jr., and Bruns, Rogers (eds.). Congress Investigates: 1792-1974. New York: Chelsea House Publishers. 1975 (5 Vols.).

JK1123.A2S34

Shampansky, Jay R. Staff Depositions in Congressional Investigations. CRS Report 95-949 A, December 3, 1999.

_____. Congress' Contempt Power. CRS Report 86-83A, February 28, 1986.

Shane, Peter M. Legal Disagreement and Negotiation in a Government of Laws: The Case of Executive Privilege Claims Against Congress. Minnesota Law Review, v. 71, February 1987: 461.

Shane, Peter M. Negotiation for Knowledge: Administrative Responses to congressional Demands for Information. Administrative Law Review, v. 44, Spring 1992: 197.

Stathis, Stephen W. Executive Cooperation: Presidential Recognition of the Investigative Authority of Congress and the Courts. Journal of Law and Politics, v. 3, Fall 1986: 187.

Taylor, Teleford. Grand Inquest: The Story of Congressional Investigations. New York: Simon and Schuster, 1995.

                                                                                KF4942.T38

Tiefer, Charles. Congressional Oversight of the Clinton Administration and Congressional Procedure. Administrative Law Review, v. 50, 1998: 199.

Walsh, Lawrence E. The Independent Counsel and the Separation of Powers. Houston Law Review, v. 25, January 1988:1.

APPENDIX A
Illustrative Subpoena

Subpena Duces Tecum

By Authority of the House of Representatives of the Congress of the United States of America

To ..Custodian.of.Documents.International.Brotherhood.of.Teamsters.............

You are hereby commanded to produce the things identified on the attached schedule before the Subcommittee on Oversight and.Investigations. Committee on ..Education.and.the.Workforce............

of the House of Representatives of the United States, of which the Hon. .Pete.Hoekstra...........

...............,................... is chairman, by producing such things in Room ...B-346A... of the

........Rayburn.............. Building ...., in the city of Washington, on

........March..17,.1998......, at the hour of ....5:00.p.m................

To .Any.staff.member.or.agent.of.the.Committee.on.Education.and.the.Workfor of.the.age.of.18.years.or.older.or.to.any.United.States.Marshal to serve and make return.

Witness my hand and the seal of the House of Representatives

of the United States, at the city of Washington, this

.....19th..... day of ....March................, 19..98...

Peter Hoekstra
....
The Honorable Pete Hoekstra   *Chairman.*

Attest:

Robin H Carle
....
Clerk.

Subpena for Custodian of Documents

International Brotherhood of Teamsters

25 Louisiana Avenue, N.W.

Washington, D.C. 20001

before the Committee on the Education

and the Workforce, Subcommittee on

Oversight and Investigations

Served

House of Representatives

General Instructions

1. In complying with this Subpoena, you are required to produce all responsive documents that are in your possession, custody, or control, whether held by you or your past or present agents, employees, and representatives acting on your behalf. You are also required to produce documents that you have a legal right to obtain, documents that you have a right to copy or have access to, and documents that you have placed in the temporary possession, custody, or control of any third party. No records, documents, data or information called for by this requires shall be destroyed, modified, removed or otherwise made inaccessible to the Committee.

2. In the event that any entity, organization or individual denoted in this subpoena has been, or is also known by any other name than that herein denoted, the subpoena shall be read to also include them under that alternative identification.

3. Each document produced shall be produced in a form that renders the document susceptible of copying.

4. Documents produced in response to this subpoena shall be produced together with copies of file labels, dividers or identifying markers with which they were associated when this subpoena was served. Also identify to which paragraph from the subpoena that such documents are responsive.

5. It shall not be a basis for refusal to produce documents that any other person or entity also possesses non-identical or identical copies of the same document.

6. If any of the subpoenaed information is available in machine-readable form (such as punch cards, paper or magnetic tapes, drums, disks, or core storage), state the form in which it is available and provide sufficient detail to allow the information to be copied to a readable format. If the information requested is stored in a computer, indicate whether you have an existing program that will print the records in a readable form.

7. If the subpoena cannot be complied with in full, it shall be complied with to the extent possible, which shall include an explanation of why full compliance is not possible.

8. In the event that a document is withheld on the basis of privilege, provide the following information concerning any such document: (a) the privilege asserted; (b) the type of document; (c) the general subject matter; (d) the date, author and addressee; and (e) the relationship of the author and addressee to each other.

9. If any document responsive tot his subpoena was, but no longer is, in your possession, custody or control, identify the document (stating its date, author, subject and recipients) and explain the circumstances by which the document ceased to be in your possession, or control.

10. If a date set forth in this subpoena referring to a communication, meeting, or other event is inaccurate, but the actual date is known to you or is otherwise apparent from the context of the request, you should produce all documents which would be responsive as if the date were correct.

11. Other than subpoena questions directed at the activities of specified entities or persons, to the extent that information contained in documents sought by this subpoena may require production of donor lists, or information otherwise enabling the re-creation of donor lists, such identifying information may be redacted.

12. The time period covered by this subpoena is included in the attached Schedule A.

13. This request is continuing in nature. Any record, document, compilation of data or information, not produced because it has not been located or discovered by the return date, shall be produced immediately upon location or discovery subsequent thereto.

14. All documents shall be Bates stamped sequentially and produced sequentially.

15. Two sets of documents shall be delivered, one set for the Majority Staff and one set for the Minority Staff. When documents are produced to the Subcommittee, production sets shall be delivered to the Majority Staff in Room B346 Rayburn House Office Building and the Minority Staff in Room 2101 Rayburn House Office Building.

General Definitions

1. The term "document" means any written, recorded, or graphic matter of any nature whatsoever, regardless of how recorded, and whether original or copy, including, but not limited to, the following: memoranda, reports, expense reports, books, manuals, instructions, financial reports, working papers, records notes, letters, notices, confirmations, telegrams, receipts, appraisals, pamphlets, magazines, newspapers, prospectuses, interoffice and intra office communications, electronic mail (E-mail), contracts, cables, notations of any type of conversation, telephone call, meeting or other communication, bulletins, printed matter, computer printouts, teletypes, invoices, transcripts, diaries, analyses, returns, summaries, minutes, bills, accounts, estimates, projections, comparisons, messages, correspondence, press releases, circulars, financial statements, reviews, opinions, offers, studies and investigations, questionnaires and surveys, and work sheets (and all drafts, preliminary versions, alterations, modifications, revisions, changes, and amendments of any of the foregoing, as well as any attachments or appendices thereto), and graphic or oral records or representations of any kind (including without limitation, photographs, charts, graphs, microfiche, microfilm, videotape, recordings and motion pictures), and electronic, mechanical, and electric records or representations of any kind (including, without limitation, tapes, cassettes, discs, and recordings) and other written, printed, typed, or other graphic or recorded matter of any kind or nature, however produced or reproduced, and whether preserved in writing, film, tape, disc, or videotape. A documents bearing any notation not a part of the original text is to be considered a separate document. A draft or non-identical copy is a separate document within the meaning of this term.

2. The term "communication" means each manner or means of disclosure or exchange of information, regardless of information, regardless of means utilized, whether oral, electronic, by document or otherwise, and whether face to face, in a meeting, by telephone, mail, telexes, discussions, releases, personal delivery, or otherwise.

3. The terms "and" and "or" shall be construed broadly and either conjunctively or disjunctively to bring within the scope of this subpoena any information which might otherwise be construed to be outside its scope. The singular includes plural number, and vice versa. The masculine includes the feminine and neuter genders.

4. The term "White House" refers to the executive Office of the President and all of its units including, without limitation, the Office of Administration, the White House Office, the Office of the Vice President, the Office of the Science and Technology Policy, the Office of Management and Budget, the United States Trade Representative, the Office of Public Liaison, the Office of Correspondence, the Office of the Deputy Chief of Staff for Policy and Political Affairs, the Office of the Deputy Chief of Staff for White House Operations, the Domestic Policy Council, the Office of Federal Procurement Policy, the Office of Intergovernmental Affairs, the Office of Legislative Affairs, Media Affairs, the National Economic Council, the Office of Policy Development, the Office of Political Affairs, the Office of

Presidential Personnel, the Office of the Press Secretary, the Office of Scheduling and Advance, the Council for Economic Advisors, the Council on Environmental Quality, the Executive Residence, the President's Foreign Intelligence Advisory Board, the National Security Council, the Office of National Drug Control, and the Office of Policy Development.

March 10, 1998

Custodian of Documents
International Brotherhood of Teamsters
25 Louisiana Avenue, N.W.
Washington, D.C. 2001

SCHEDULE A

1. All organizational charts and personnel rosters for the International Brotherhood of Teamsters ("Teamsters" or "IBT"), including the DRIVE PAC, in effect during calendar years 1991 through 1997.

2. All IBT operating, finance, and administrative *manuals* in effect during calendar years 1991 through 1997, including, but not limited to those that set forth (1) operating policies, practices, and procedures; (2) internal financial practices and reporting requirements; and (3) authorization, approval, and review responsibilities.

3. All annual audit reports of the IBT for the years 1991 through 1996 performed by the auditing firm of Grant Thornton.

4. All IBT annual reports to its membership and the public for years 1991 through 1997, including copies of IBT annual audited financial statements certified to by independent public accountants.

5. All books and records showing receipts and expenditures, assets and liabilities, profits and losses, and all other records used for recording the financial affairs of the IBT including, journals (or other books of original entry) and ledgers including cash receipts journals, cash disbursements journals, revenue journals, general journals, subledgers, and work papers reflecting accounting entries.

6. All Federal Income Tax returns filed by the IBT for years 1991 through 1997.

7. All minutes of the General Board, Executive Board, Executive Council, and all Standing Committees, including any internal ethics committees formed to investigate misconduct and corruption, and all handouts and reports prepared and produced at each Committee meeting.

8. All documents referring or relating to, or containing information about, any contribution, donation, expenditure, outlay, in-kind assistance, transfer, loan, or grant (from DRIVE, DRIVE E&L fund, or IBT general treasury) to any of the following entities/ organizations:

    a. Citizen Action
    b. Campaign for a Responsible Congress

     c. Project Vote
     d. National Council of Senior Citizens
     e. Vote Now '96
     f. AFL-CIO
     g. AFSCMS
     h. Democratic National Committee
     i. Democratic Senatorial Campaign Committee ("DSCC")
     j. Democratic Congressional Campaign Committee ("DCCC")
     k. State Democratic Parties
     l. Clinton-Gore '96
     m. SEIU

9. All documents referring or relating to, or containing information about any of the following individuals/entities:

     a. Teamsters for a Corruption Free Union
     b. Teamsters for a Democratic Union
     c. Concerned Teamsters 2000
     d. Martin Davis
     e. Michael Ansara
     f. Jerre Nash
     g. Sahre Group
     h. November Group
     i. Terrence McAuliffe
     j. Charles Blitz
     k. New Party
     l. James P. Hoffa Campaign
     m. Delancy Printing
     n. Axis Enterprises
     o. Barbara Arnold
     p. Peter McGourty
     q. Charles McDonald
     r. Theodore Kheel

10. All documents referring or relating to, or containing information on about, communications between the Teamsters and the White House regarding any of the following issues:

     a. United Parcel Service Strike
     b. Diamond Walnut Company Strike
     c. Pony Express Company organizing efforts
     d. Davis Bacon Act
     e. NAFTA Border Crossings
     f. Ron Carey reelection campaign
     g. IBT support to 1996 federal election campaigns

h. All documents referring or relating to, or containing information about, communications between the Teamsters and the Federal Election Commission.

12. All documents referring or relating to, or containing information about, communications between the Teamsters and the Democratic National Committee, DSCC, or DCCC.

13. All documents referring or relating to, or containing information about, communications between the Teamsters and the Clinton-Gore '96 Campaign Committee.

14. All documents referring or relating to, or containing information about, policies and procedures in effect during 1996 regarding the approval of expenditures from the IBT general treasury, DRV E&L fund, and DRIVE PAC.

15. All documents referring or relating to, or containing information about the retention by the IBT of the law firm Covington & Burling and/or Charles Ruff.

16. All documents referring or relating to, or containing information about work for the IBT performed by the firm Palladino & Sutherland and/or Jack Palladino.

17. All documents referring or relating to, or containing information about work for the IBT performed by Ace investigations and/or Gueerieri, Edmund, and James.

18. All documents referring or relating to, or containing information about IBT involvement in the 1995-1996 Oregon Senate race (Ron Wyden vs. Gordon Smith).

19. All documents referring or relating to, or containing information about, Ron Carey's campaign for reelection as general president of the Teamsters.

20. All documents referring or relating to, or containing information about organization, planning, and operation of the 1996 IBT Convention.

21. All documents referring or relating to, or containing information about the following:

    a. Trish Hoppey
    b. John Latz
    c. Any individual with the last name of "Golovner".
    d. Convention Management Group.

22. All documents referring or relating to, or containing information about the Household Finance Corporation.

23. All documents referring or relating to, or containing information about, any "affinity credit card" program or other credit card program sponsored by or participated in by the IBT.

24. A list of all bank accounts held by the International Brotherhood of Teamsters including the name of the bank, account number, and bank address.

25. All documents referring or relating to, or containing information about, payments made by the IBT to any official or employee of the Independent Review Board.

26. Unless otherwise indicated, the time period covered by this subpoena is between January 1991 and December 1997.

APPENDIX B

THE WHITE HOUSE
November 4, 1982

MEMORANDUM FOR THE HEADS OF EXECUTIVE DEPARTMENTS AND AGENCIES

SUBJECT: Procedures Governing Responses to
          Congressional Request for Information

The policy of this administration is to comply with Congressional Requests for information to the fullest extent consistent with the constitutional and statutory obligations of the Executive Branch. While this Administration, like its predecessors, has an obligation to protect the confidentiality of some communications, executive privilege will be asserted only in the most compelling circumstances, and only after careful review demonstrates that assertion of the privilege is necessary. Historically, good faith negotiations between Congress and the executive branch has minimized the need for invoking executive privilege, and this tradition of accommodation should continue as the primary means of resolving conflicts between the Branches. To ensure that every reasonable accommodation is made to the needs of Congress, executive privilege shall not be invoked without specific Presidential authorization.

The Supreme Court has held that the Executive Branch may occasionally find it necessary and proper to preserve the confidentiality of national security secrets, deliberative communications that form a part of the decision-making process, or other information important to the discharge of the Executive Branch's constitutional responsibilities. Legitimate and appropriate claims of privilege should not thoughtlessly be waived. However, to ensure that this Administration acts responsibly and consistently in the exercise of its duties, with due regard for the responsibilities and prerogatives of Congress, the following procedures shall be followed whenever Congressional requests for information raise concerns regarding the confidentiality of the information sought:

1. Congressional requests for information shall be complied with as promptly and as fully as possible, unless it is determined that compliance raises a substantial question of executive privilege. A "substantial question of executive privilege" exists if disclosure of the information requested might significantly impair the national security *including the conduct of foreign relations), the deliberative processes of the Executive Branch or other aspects of the performance of the Executive Branch's constitutional duties.

2. If the head of an executive department or agency ("Department Head") believes, after consultation with department counsel, that compliance with a Congressional request for information raises a substantial question of executive privilege, he shall promptly notify and consult with the Attorney General through the Assistant Attorney General for the Office of Legal Counsel, and shall also promptly notify and consult with the Counsel to the President. If the information requested of a department or agency derives in whole or in part or from information received from another department or agency, the latter entity shall also be consulted as to whether disclosure of the information raises a substantial question of executive privilege.

3. Every effort shall be made to comply with the Congressional request in a manner consistent with the legitimate needs of the Executive Branch. The Department Head, the Attorney "General and the Counsel to the President may, in the exercise of their

discretion in the circumstances, determine that executive privilege shall not be invoked and release the requested information.

4. If the Department Head, the Attorney General or the Counsel to the President believes, after consultation, that the circumstances justify invocation of executive privilege, the issue shall be presented to the President by the Counsel to the President, who will advise the Department Head and the Attorney General of the President's decision.

5. Pending a final Presidential decision on the matter, the Department Head shall request the Congressional body to hold its request for the information in abeyance. The Department Head shall expressly indicate that the purpose of this request is to protect the privilege pending a Presidential decision, claim of privilege.

6. If the President decides to invoke executive privilege, the Department Head shall advise the requesting Congressional body that the claim of executive privilege is being made with the specific approval of the President.

Any questions concerning these procedures or related matters should be addressed to the Attorney General, through the Assistant Attorney General for the Office of Legal Counsel, and to the Counsel to the President.

· Ronald Reagan

APPENDIX C

THE WHITE HOUSE

September 28, 1994

MEMORANDUM FOR ALL EXECUTIVE DEPARTMENT AND AGENCY GENREAL COUNSELS

FROM: LLOYD N. CUTLER, SPECIAL COUNSEL TO THE PRESIDENT

SUBJECT: Congressional Requests to Departments and Agencies for Documents Protected by Executive Privilege

The policy of this Administration is to comply with congressional requests for information to the fullest extent consistent with the constitutional and statutory obligations of the Executive Branch. While this Administration, like its predecessors, has an obligation to protect the confidentiality of core communications, executive privilege will be asserted only after careful review demonstrates that assertion of the privilege is necessary to protect Executive Branch prerogatives.

The doctrine of executive privilege protects the confidentiality of deliberations within the White House, including its policy councils, as well as communications between the White House and executive departments and agencies. Executive privilege applies to written and oral communications between and among the white House, its policy councils and Executive Branch agencies, as well as to documents that describe or prepares for such communications (e.g., "talking points"). This has been the view expressed by all recent White House Counsels. In circumstances involving communications relating to investigations of personal wrongdoing by government officials, it is our practice not to assert executive privilege, either, in judicial proceedings or in congressional investigations and hearings. Executive privilege must always be weighed against other competing governmental interests, including the judicial need to obtain relevant evidence, especially in criminal proceedings, and the congressional need to make factual findings for legislative and oversight purposes.

In the last resort, this balancing is usually conducted by the courts. However, when executive privilege is asserted against a congressional request for documents, the courts usually decline to intervene until after the other two branches have exhausted the possibility of working out a satisfactory accommodation. It is our policy to work out such an accommodation whenever we can, without unduly interfering with the President's need to conduct frank exchange of views with h is principal advisors.

Historically, good faith negotiations between Congress and the Executive Branch have minimized the need for invoking executive privilege.

Executive privilege belongs to the President, not individual departments or agencies. It is essential that all requests to departments and agencies for information of the type described above be referred to the White House Counsel before any information is furnished. Departments and agencies receiving such request should therefore follow the procedures set forth below, designed to ensure that this Administration acts responsibly and consistently with respect to executive privilege issues, with due regard for the responsibilities and prerogatives of Congress:

<u>First</u>, any document created in the White House, including a White House policy council, or in a department or agency, that contains the deliberations of, or advice to or from the White House, should be presumptively treated as protected by executive privilege. This is so regardless of the document's location at the time of the request or whether it originated in the White House or in a department or agency.

<u>Second</u>, a department or agency receiving a request for any such document should promptly notify the White House Counsel's Office, and direct any inquiries regarding such a document to the White House Counsel's Office.

<u>Third</u>, the White House Counsel's Office, working together with the department or agency (and, where appropriate, the Department of justice), will discuss the request with appropriate congressional representatives to determine whether a mutually satisfactory recommendation is available.

<u>Fourth</u>, if efforts to reach a mutually satisfactory accommodation are unsuccessful, and if release of the documents would pass a substantial question of executive privilege, the counsel to the President will consult with the Department of Justice and other affected agencies to determine whether to recommend that the President invoke the privilege.

We believe this policy will facilitate the resolution of issues relating to disclosures to Congress and maximize the opportunity for reaching mutually satisfactory accommodations with Congress. We will of course try to cooperate with reasonable congressional requests for information in ways that preserve the President's ability to exchange frank advice with is immediate staff and the heads of the executive departments and agencies.

IV. SELECTED OVERSIGHT TECHNIQUES

Many oversight techniques are self-explanatory. There are several techniques, however, for which explanation or elaboration may prove helpful for a better understanding of their utility.

A. DETERMINE LAWS, PROGRAMS, ACTIVITIES, FUNCTIONS, ADVISORY COMMITTEES, AGENCIES, AND DEPARTMENTS WITHIN EACH COMMITTEE'S JURISDICTION

A basic step in oversight preparation is to determine the laws, programs, activities, functions, advisory committees, agencies, and departments within a committee's jurisdiction. This is essential if a committee is to know the full range of its oversight responsibilities. To accomplish this general goal, House and Senate committees might:

1. Prepare a document as needed, which outlines for each subcommittee of a standing committee the agencies, laws, programs activities, functions, advisory committees, and required agency reports that fall within its jurisdiction purview.

2. Publish, as needed, a compilation of all the basic statutes in force within the jurisdiction of each subcommittee or for the committee itself if it has no subcommittees.

3. Request the assistance of the various legislative support agencies (the Congressional Budget Office, the Congressional Research Service, or the General Accounting Office) in identifying the full range of federal programs and activities under a committee's jurisdiction.

B. ORIENTATION AND PERIODIC REVIEW HEARINGS WITH AGENCIES

1. Oversight hearings (or even 'pre-hearings") may be held for the purposes of briefing Members and staff on the organization, operations, and programs of an agency, and determining how an agency intends to implement any new legislation. The hearings can also be used as a way to obtain information on the administration, effectiveness, and economy of agency operations and programs.

2. Agency officials can be noticeably influenced by the knowledge and expectation that they will be called before a congressional committee regularly to account for the activities of their agencies.

3. Such hearings benefit the committee by, for example:

    a. helping committee members keep up-to-date on important administrative developments;

    b. serving as a forum for exchanging and communicating views on pertinent problems and other relevant matters;

    c. providing background information which could assist members in making sound legislative and fiscal judgments;

    d. identifying program areas within each committee's jurisdiction that may be vulnerable to waste, fraud, abuse, or mismanagement; and

    e. determining whether new laws are needed or whether changes in the administration of existing laws will be sufficient to resolve problems.

4. The ability of committee members during oversight hearings to focus on meaningful issues and to ask penetrating questions will be enhanced if staffs have accumulated, organized, and evaluated relevant data, information, and analyses about administrative performance.

    a. Ideally, each standing committee should regularly monitor the application of laws and implementation of programs within its jurisdiction. A prime objective of the "continuous watchfulness" mandate (Section 136) of the Legislative Reorganization Act of 1946 is to encourage committees to take an active and ongoing role in administrative review and not wait for public revelations of agency and program inadequacies before conducting oversight. As Section 136 states in part: "each standing committee of the Senate and Hoes of Representatives shall exercise continuous watchfulness of the execution by the administrative agencies concerned of any laws, the subject matter of which is within the jurisdiction of such committee."

b.   Committee personnel could be assigned to maintain active liaison with appropriate agencies and to record their pertinent findings routinely.

c.   Information compiled in this fashion will be useful not only for regular oversight hearings, but also for oversight hearings called unexpectedly with little opportunity to conduct an extensive background study.

5.   It is important that specific letters be directed by the committee to the agency witnesses so that they will be on notice about what they will have to answer. In this way witnesses will be responsive in providing worthwhile testimony at hearings; testify "to the point" and avoid rambling and/or evasive statements; and restrict their use of this kind of answer to questions: "I didn't know you wanted that information…"

C. CASEWORK

An important check against bureaucratic indifference or inefficiency is "casework," as noted in Section I. Typically, Members of Congress hear from individual constituents and communities about problems they are having with various federal agencies and departments. As a House member once said:

> Last year, one of my constituents, a 63-year old man who requires kidney dialysis, discovered that he would no longer be receiving Medicare because the Social Security Administration thought he was dead. Like many residents who have problems dealing with the federal bureaucracy, this man contacted my district office and asked for help. Without difficulty, he convinced my staff that he was indeed alive, and we in turn convinced the Social Security Administration to resume sending him benefits.[61]

Casework is important only in resolving problems that constituents are having with bureaucrats but also in identifying limitations in the law. As a scholar of constituency service explained: "Casework allows ad hoc correction of bureaucratic error, impropriety, and laxity, and can lead a senator or representative to consider changes in laws because of particularly flagrant or persistent problems that casework staff discovered."[62]

D. AUDITS

1.   *Periodic auditing* of executive departments is among the strongest techniques of legislative oversight. Properly utilized, the audit enables Congress to hold executive officers to a strict accounting for their use of public funds and the conduct of their administration.

---

[61] Lee H. Hamilton, "Constituent Service and Representation," *The Public Manager,* Summer 1992, p. 12.

[62] John R. Johannes, "Constituency Service," in Donald Bacon, *et al.,* eds., *The Encyclopedia of the United States Congress,* New York: Simon and Schuster, 1995, p. 544.

2. *Government auditing* encompasses more than checking and verifying accounts, and financial statements. Many federal, state, and some foreign audit agencies are moving in the direction pioneered by GAO (the chief audit agency of Congress) of including an evaluation of:

    a. whether claimed *achievements* are *supported* by adequate and reliable evidence and data and are in compliance with legislatively established objectives; and

    b. whether resources are being used efficiently, effectively, and economically.

3. In reviewing the agencies' own evaluations, or in undertaking an initial evaluation, auditors are advised by GAO to ask questions such as the following:

    a. How successful is the program in *accomplishing the intended results?* Could program objectives be achieved at less cost?

    b. Has agency management clearly defined and promulgated the objectives and goals of the program or activity?

    c. Have *performance standards been developed?*

    d. Are *program objectives* sufficiently clear to permit agency management to accomplish effectively the desired program results? Are the objectives of the component parts of the program consistent with overall program objectives?

    e. Are program costs reasonably commensurate with the benefits achieved?

    f. *Have alternative programs or approaches been examined,* or should they be examined to determine whether objectives can be achieved more economically?

    g. Were all studies, such as cost-benefit studies, appropriate for analyzing costs and benefits of alternative approaches?

    h. Is the program producing benefits or detriments that were not contemplated by Congress when it authorized the program?

    i. Is the *information furnished* to Congress by the agency *adequate and sufficiently accurate* to permit Congress to monitor program achievements effectively?

    j. Does top management have *the essential and reliable information* necessary for exercising supervision and control and for ascertaining directions or trends?

    k. Does management have *internal review or audit facilities* adequate for monitoring program operations, identifying program and management problems and weaknesses, and insuring fiscal integrity?

4. In addition to GAO and other governmental audits, Congress may have access to the internal audit reports of agency audit teams.

a. Internal audit reports are designed to meet the needs of *executive* officials.

b. This information is useful in conducting oversight; executive agencies are sometimes reluctant to provide internal audit reports to Congress.

c. A large number of governmental and private organizations conduct audits of expenditures. Every major federal agency, for example, has its own statutory Inspector General and each of the 50 states plus hundreds of local governments have their own audit offices. Many government agencies also contract with public accounting firms to perform financial audits. For assistance in finding audit reports or in learning how to commission audit reports, congressional staff might consult with officials at the GAO, which is the auditing arm of the Congress.

E. MONITORING THE *FEDERAL REGISTER*

1. The Federal Register is published daily, Monday through Friday, except official holidays by the Office of the Federal Register, National Archives and Records Administration. It provides a uniform system for making available to the public regulations and legal notices issued by Federal agencies. These include presidential proclamations and executive orders, federal agency documents having general applicability and legal effect, documents required to be published by act of Congress, and other Federal agency documents of public interest. Final regulations are codified by subject in the Code of Federal Regulations.

2. Documents are on file for public inspection in the Office of the Federal Register the day before they are published, unless the issuing agency requests earlier filing. The list of documents on file for public inspection can be accessed via www.nara.gov/fedreg.

3. Regular scrutiny of the Federal Register by committees and staff may help them to identify proposed rules and regulations in their subject areas that merit congressional review as to need and likely effect.

4. The Federal Register is now available and searchable online (see www.acess.gpo.gov/nara). The Regulatory Information Service Center of the General Services Administration annually issues two publications – the *Unified Agenda of Federal Regulatory and Deregulatory Actions* in April and *The Regulatory Plan and the Unified Agenda of Federal Regulatory and Deregulatory Actions* in October – that provide a wealth of information about proposed and completed regulatory actions of federal agencies. Both documents are available online (http://reginfo.gov). Further information about these two publications can be obtained from the Center. The Center's telephone number is (202) 482-7350 and its e-mail address is RIS@gsa.gov.

F. SPECIAL STUDIES AND INVESTIGATIONS BY STAFF, SUPPORT AGENCIES, OUTSIDE CONTRACTORS, AND OTHERS

1. *Staff Investigations.* The staffs of committees and individual Members play a vital role in the legislative process.

   a. Committee staffs, through field investigations or on-site visits for example, can help a committee develop its own independent evaluation of the effectiveness of laws.

2. *Support Agencies.* The legislative support agencies, directly or indirectly, can assist committees and Members in conducting investigations and reviewing agency performance. (See Section V for a discussion of CRS, GAO, and CBO capabilities.)

   a. The General Accounting Office is the agency most involved in investigations, audits, and program evaluations. It has a large, professional investigative staff and produces numerous reports useful in oversight.

3. *Outside Contractors.* The 1974 Budget Act, as amended and the Legislative Reorganization Act of 1970 authorize House and Senate committees to enlist the services of individual consultants or organizations to assist them in their work.

   a. A committee might contract with an independent research organization or employ professional investigators for short-term studies.

   b. Committees may also utilize, subject to appropriate approvals, federal and support agency employees to aid them in their oversight activities.

   c. Committees might also establish a voluntary advisory panel to assist them in their work.

G. COMMUNICATING WITH THE MEDIA

1. Public exposure of a problem is an effective oversight technique, and will often help bring about a solution to that problem. Public officials often seem much more responsive to correcting deficiencies *after* the issue has been described in widely circulated news stories.

2. Effective communication with the media is based on knowledge and understanding of each of the media forms and the *advantages* and *disadvantages* of each.

A. Wire Services

(1) Timeliness, brevity, and accuracy are the main criteria for dealing with the wire service.

(2) Personal contact with wire service reporters gets the best results.

B. Daily Newspapers

(1) Obtain information on the operational procedures and deadlines of daily newspapers, and how they are affected by time.

(2) Since regular news for Monday is usually low, it may be useful to issue statements and releases for "Monday a.m." use.

(3) Saturday usually has the lowest circulation and Sunday has the widest.

(4) Stories for weekend publication should be given to reporters during the middle of the week or earlier.

C. Magazines

(1) Magazines and other periodicals are generally wider ranging and focus on why something happens, not *what* happened.

(2) Weeklies do not ordinarily respond to Member press conferences and releases in the same manner as the other media; personal meetings and telephone conversations are usually more effective.

(3) *Deadlines Vary*

    (a) Obtain information on operational procedures.
    (b) Weekends are generally production periods for most magazines.

D. Trade Periodicals

Many of these topically oriented magazines and newsletters are produced by publishing firms, which utilize the services of the periodical press galleries in the Capitol.

E. Television

(1) House and Senate rules identify procedures for radio and television broadcasting of committee hearings. (See Hoes Rule XI and Senate Rule XXVI).

(2) News of a committee's oversight activities may appear in diverse forms on television. For example, it could appear on the networks as a brief report on the morning or evening news, air on a cable news channel, or arise in the course of live House or Senate floor debate telecast over C-SPAN (the Cable Satellite Public Affairs Network).

Washington-based news organizations may also provide daily television coverage of congress to independent television stations. Public television and cable news organizations occasionally broadcast live coverage of committee oversight hearings.

(3) To encourage television coverage of a committee's oversight activities, the following checklist might be helpful to staff.

(a) Alert correspondents and Washington bureau chiefs of upcoming hearings several days in advance via press releases; follow up with personal or telephone notification of certain "must-contact" correspondents.

(b) Notify the Associated Press, Reuters, and other news services of a scheduled hearing or meeting at least a day in advance. Allow enough lead-time to permit inclusion of the committee activity in the wire services' calendar of daily events for the next day.

(c) If widespread media interest is anticipated, reserve at least a week in advance a hearing room large enough to accommodate televisions cameras.

(d) Alert interested correspondents or assignment editors when House or Senate floor action is likely on a matter related to the committee's oversight function.

(e) Provide or have available for the media background information on oversight issues awaiting committee action or consideration by the House or Senate.

(f) Consider making committee members readily available for television cameras either before or after any executive sessions (*e.g.,* allowing television crews in briefly at the start to take video footage of the committee, or arranging for a press conference after the committee session).

(g) Videotape, where appropriate committee members discussing topical oversight issues for distribution to interested television stations.

(h) Keep the contact person of each of the network news interview programs ("Meet the Press," etc.) apprized of a committee's oversight activities, and their relevance to topical national issues. Suggest the appearance of committee members on interview programs when a committee oversight issue becomes especially newsworthy.

(i) Be alert to live television interview possibilities for committee members that can be arranged on relatively short notice, *e.g.,* newsmaker interviews on cable news channels.

F. Radio

(1) Time is of the essence. Radio newsmen want congressional reaction *immediately,* not hours later when the story breaks in the newspaper or on television.

(2) Members who are readily available for quick interviews are frequently broadcast within minutes or the next morning coast-to-coast on hundreds of radio stations. In most cases an interview will be aired repeatedly over a period of several hours.

(3) Congressional offices should contact radio reporters *directly* through the House and Senate press galleries.

G. Press Conferences

(1) *Time*

  (a) The periods between 10 a.m. and 2 p.m. are often preferable.

  (b) *Early* morning press conferences usually have low attendance because reporters on daily papers do not start work until mid-morning.

  (c) Late afternoon press conferences are often unattended because reporters begin to lose news time for that particular day.

  (d) Check with the press galleries. They keep a running log of most scheduled news events and can provide information on possible competition at any time on any day.

(2) *Place*

  (a) Committee rooms are good, but they are frequently in use at the best time for a conference.

(b) A Member's office or the press galleries can be adequate, but keep in mind that the reporter and cameramen need room to operate.

(c) It might be wise to go to the radio-TV galleries after the conference and do a repeat to get electronic coverage.

(3) *Notification*

(a) Notify the press galleries in *writing* as far in advance as possible.

(b) Also notify the wire services and television networks *directly at their downtown offices.*

(4) *Form*

(a) A press conference should be viewed as an open house with *everybody* invited and *everybody* welcome.

(b) A brief *opening* statement should be read or summarized. After copies of it have been distributed, the questioning should begin.

(1) leave plenty of time for questions.
(2) Do not restrict the areas of questioning.
(3) Anticipate the questions and have answers prepared.

(c) The normal time for a routine press conference is about one-half hour.

H. News Releases

(1) A good news release answers in *one page* or less the questions where, when, who, what, how, why, and, for some topics, how much (*e.g.,* cost) or how many *(e.g.,* beneficiaries).

(2) A good news release should:

(a) Contain the name, *telephone number*, and e-mail of your *press contact*;

(b) Be for *immediate* release (better than embargo);

(c) Quote the Member *directly;*

(d) Avoid excessive use of the Member's name;

(e) Avoid needles big words, *long* sentences, and *long* paragraphs; and

(f) Make the point quickly, clearly, directly, and then end.

I. The Internet and the Media

(1) Members and committees can use the Internet to communicate with media representatives and constituents to explain their views and positions with respect to oversight activities. The Internet permits lawmakers and committees to rely less on traditional journalistic sources for coverage and more on direct communication with the citizenry.

(2) The Internet can be employed in a variety of ways to mobilize public interest in congressional oversight. For example, lawmakers can conduct on-line discussions with interested citizens or committees can establish their own World Wide Web sites to solicit input form individuals and organizations about executive branch departments and programs.

H. STATUTORY OFFICES OF INSPECTOR GENERAL

Statutory offices of inspector general consolidate responsibility for auditing and investigations within a federal department, agency, or other organization. Established by public law as permanent, nonpartisan, independent offices, they now exist in nearly 60 federal establishments and entities, including all departments and the largest agencies as well as many smaller boards, commissions, and governmental corporations. Under two major enactments -- the Inspector General Act of 1978 and its amendments of 1988 – the inspectors general (IGs) have been granted a substantial amount of independence and authority to carry out their basic mandate to combat waste, fraud, and abuse, now including the use of their personnel in counter-terrorism efforts. Recent statutes, moreover, have added a new IG for Tax Administration in Treasury; converted the IG in the Tennessee Valley Authority to a presidential appointment subject to Senate confirmation; consolidated some foreign policy agencies into the State Department, thus ending their separate IG offices; and created a Criminal Investigator Academy and an Inspector General Forensic Laboratory.

Responsibilities

Inspectors general have three principal responsibilities under the Inspector General Act of 1978, as amended:

- conducting and supervising audits and investigations relating to the programs and operations of the establishment.
- Providing leadership and cooperation and recommending policies for activities designed to promote the economy, efficiency, and effectiveness of such programs and operations, and preventing and detecting fraud and abuse in such programs and operations; and
- Providing a means for keeping the establishment head and Congress fully and currently informed about problems and deficiencies relating to the administration of

such programs and operations, and the necessity for and progress of corrective action.

Authority and Duties

To carry out the purposes of the Inspector General Act, IGs have been granted broad authority to conduct audits and investigations; access directly all records and information of the agency; request assistance from other federal, state, and local government agencies; subpoena information and documents; administer oaths when taking testimony; hire staff and manage their own resources; and receive and respond to complaints from agency employees, whose confidentiality is to be protected. Also, beginning in 1996, most IGs in the federal establishments were granted police powers via special deputation authority from the Justice Department. In the aftermath of the terrorist attacks on the Pentagon and World Trade Center on September 11, 2001, moreover, IG staff have been redeployed to assist in airline security and in terrorist investigations by the FBI and other agencies.

Notwithstanding these powers and duties, IGs are not authorized to take corrective action or make any reforms themselves. Indeed, the Inspector General Act, as amended, prohibits the transfer of "program operating responsibilities" to an IG (5 U.S.C. Appendix 3, Section 9(a)(2)). The rationale for this prohibition is that it would be difficult, if not impossible, for Igs to audit or investigate programs and operations impartially and objectively if they were directly involved in carrying them out.

Reporting Requirements

IGs also have important obligations concerning their findings, conclusions, and recommendations for corrective action. These include reporting (1) suspected violations of federal criminal law directly and expeditiously to the Attorney General; (2) semiannually to the agency head, who must submit the IG report (along with his or her comments) to Congress within 30 days; and (3) "particularly serious or flagrant problems" immediately to the agency head, who must submit the IG report (along with comments) to Congress within seven days. The IG for the Central Intelligence Agency (CIA), operating under a different statute, must also report to the House and Senate Select Committees on Intelligence if the Director (or Acting Director of Central Intelligence is the focus of an investigation, audit, or inspection.

By means of these reports and "otherwise," IGs are to keep the agency head and Congress fully and currently informed. Other informing activities include testifying at congressional hearings; meeting with legislators, officials, and staff; and responding to congressional requests for information and reports.

Independence

In addition to having their own powers (e.g., to hire staff and issue subpoenas), the IGS' independent status is reinforced in a number of other ways: protection of their budgets, qualifications on their appointment and removal, prohibitions on interference with their activities and operations, and a proscription on being assigned any program operating responsibilities.

Appropriations

Presidentially appointed IGs in the larger federal agencies have a separate appropriations account (a separate budget account in the case of the CIA) for their offices. This situation prevents agency administrators from limiting, transferring, or otherwise reducing IG funding once it has been specified in law.

Appointment and Removal

Under the Inspector General Act, as amended, IGs are to be selected without regard to political affiliation and solely on the basis of integrity and demonstrated ability in accounting, auditing, financial and management analysis, law, public administration, or investigations. The CIA IG, who operates under these criteria as well as prior experience in the filed of foreign intelligence and in compliance with the security standards of the agency.

Presidentially appointed IGs in the larger federal establishments who are confirmed by the Senate can be removed only by the President. When so doing, the President must communicate the reasons for such action to Congress. However, IGs in the (usually) smaller, designated federal entities can be removed by the agency head, who must notify Congress in writing when exereising this power. In the U.S. Postal Service, by comparison, the governors appoint the inspector general – the only statutory IG with a set term (seven years). The IG can be removed with the written concurrence of at least seven of the nine governors, but only for cause – again, the only statutory IG having such a qualification governing removal.

Supervision

IGs serve under the "general supervision" of the agency head, reporting exclusively to the head or to the officer next in rank if such authority is delegated. With only a few specified exceptions, neither the agency head nor the officer next in line "shall prevent or prohibit the Inspector General from initiating, carrying out, or completing any audit or investigation, or from issuing any subpoena during the course of any audit or investigation."

Under the IG Act, as amended, the heads of three departments – Defense, Justice, and Treasury – may prevent the IG from initiating, carrying out, or completing an audit or investigation, or issuing a subpoena, in order to preserve national security interests or to protect on-going criminal investigations, among other specified reasons. When exercising this power, the department head must transmit an explanatory statement for such action to the House Government Reform and Oversight Committee, the Senate Governmental Affairs Committee, and other appropriate congressional committees and subcommittees within 30 days. Under the CIA IG Act, the Director of Central Intelligence may similarly prohibit the CIA IG from conducting investigations, audits, or inspections and, when doing so, must notify the House and Senate Intelligence Committees of the reasons for such action within seven days.

Coordination and Controls

Several presidential orders have been issued to improve coordination among the IGs and provide a means for investigating charges of wrongdoing by the IGs themselves and other top echelon officers. In early 1981, President Ronald Reagan established the President's Council on Integrity and Efficiency (PCIE) to coordinate and enhance efforts at promoting integrity and efficiency in government programs and to detect and prevent waste, fraud, and abuse (E.O.) 12301). Chaired by the Deputy Director of the Office of Management and Budget, the PCIE was composed of the existing statutory IGs plus officials from the Office of Personnel Management, the Federal Bureau of Investigation (FBI), and the Departments of Defense, Justice, and the Treasury, among others. PCIE membership was subsequently expanded to include the Controller of the Office of Federal Financial Management, the Director of the Office of Government Ethics, and the Special Counsel in the Office of Special Counsel. In 1992, following the establishment of new IG offices for various federal entities, a parallel Executive Council on Integrity and Efficiency (ECIE) was created for these new IGs and other appropriate officials. Both the PCIE and the ECIE currently operate under E.O. 12805, issued by President George Bush in 1992.

Concerns about the investigations of alleged wrongdoing by IGs themselves or other high-ranking Office of inspector General officials prompted the establishment of a new mechanism to pursue such charges. In 1996, President bill Clinton chartered an Integrity Committee, composed of PCIE and ECIE members and chaired by the FBI representative. It is to receive such allegations and, if deemed warranted, to refer them for investigation to an executive agency – including the FBI – with appropriate jurisdiction (E.O. 12993) or a special investigative unit composed of council members.

Establishment

Statutory offices of inspector general currently exist in 57 federal establishments, agencies, and entities, including all 14 cabinet departments; major executive branch agencies; independent regulatory commissions; various government corporations and foundations; and one legislative branch agency – the Government Printing Office (GPO). All but two of these offices – those in the CIA and in the GPO – are directly and explicitly under the Inspector General Act of 1978, as amended.

Each office is headed by an inspector general, who is appointed in one of two ways:

A. Nominated by the President and confirmed by the Senate in the federal establishments (i.e., all cabinet departments and the larger agencies). There are 29 of these posts (see **Table 2**); or

B. Appointed directly by the head of the entity in the designated federal entities (i.e., usually the smaller foundations, boards, commissions, and other organizations). There are 28 of these posts (see **Table 3**).

Table 2. Statutes Establishing Inspectors General Nominated by the President and Confirmed by the Senate, 1976-Present (current offices are in bold)[a]

Year	Statute	Establishment
1976	P.L.94-505	**Health, Education, and Welfare (now Health and Human Services)**
1977	P.L. 95-91	**Energy**
1978	P.L. 95-452	**Agriculture, Commerce, Housing and Urban Development, Interior, Labor, Transportation, Environmental Protection Agency, General Services, Administration, National Aeronautics and Space Administration, Small Business Administration, Veterans Administration (now the Veterans Affairs Department),** Community Services Administration[b]
1979	P.L. 96-88	**Education**
1980	P.L. 96-294	U.S. Synthetic Fuels Corporation[b]
1980	P.L. 96-465	**State[c]**
1981	P.L. 97-113	**Agency for International Development[d]**
1982	P.L. 97-252	**Defense**
1983	P.L. 98-87	**Railroad Retirement Board**
1987	P.L. 100-213	Arms Control and Disarmament Agency[b,c]
1988	P.L. 100-504	**Justice, Treasury, Federal Emergency Management Administration, Nuclear Regulatory Commission, Office of Personnel Management**
1989	P.L. 101-73	Resolution Trust Corporation[b]
1989	P.L. 101-193	**Central Intelligence Agency**
1993	P.L. 103-82	**Corporation for National and Community Service**
1993	P.L. 103-204	**Federal Deposit Insurance Corporation**
1994	P.L. 103-296	**Social Security Administration**
1994	P.L. 103-325	Community Development Financial Institutions Fund[b]
1998	P.L. 105-206	**Treasury Inspector General for Tax Administration[e]**
2000	P.L. 106-422	**Tennessee Valley Authority[f]**

[a] All, except the CIA IG, are directly under the 1978 IG Act, as amended.

[b] CSA, Synfuels Corporation, USIA, ACDA, RTC, and CDFIF have since been abolished or transferred.

[c] The State Department IG had also served as the IG for ACDA. In 1998, P.L. 105-277 abolished ACDA and USIA and transferred their functions and duties to the State Department. The Act also brought the Broadcasting Board of Governors and the International Broadcasting Bureau under the jurisdiction of the State Department IG.

[d] The IG in AID also covers the Overseas Private Investment Corporation (22 U.S.C. 2199(e)).

[e] The OIG for Tax Administration in Treasury is the only case where a separate office of inspector general exists within an establishment or entity that is otherwise covered by its own office.

[f] P.L. 106-422 also created, in the Treasury Department, a Criminal Investigator Academy to train IG staff and an Inspector General Forensic Laboratory.

Table 3. Designated Federal Entities and Agencies with Statutory IGs Appointed by the Head of the Entity or Agency (current offices are in bold)

ACTION[b]	**Government Printing Office**[f]
Amtrak	Interstate Commerce Commission[g]
Appalachian Regional Commission	**Legal Service Corporation**
Board of Governors of the Federal Reserve System	**National Archives and Records Administration**
Board for International Broadcasting[c]	**National Credit Union Administration**
Commodity Futures Trading Commission	**National Endowment for the Arts**
Consumer Product Safety Commission	**National Endowment for the Humanities**
Equal Employment Opportunity Commission	**National Science Foundation**
Farm Credit Administration	Panama Canal Commission[h]
Federal Communications Commission	**Peace Corps**
Federal Deposit Insurance Corporation[d]	**Pension Benefit Guaranty Corporation**
Federal Election Commission	**Securities and Exchange Commission**
Federal Home Loan Bank Board[e]	**Smithsonian Institution**
Federal Housing Finance Board[e]	Tennessee Valley Authority[i]
Federal Labor Relations Authority	**United States International Trade Commission**
Federal Maritime Commission	**United States Postal Service**[j]
Federal Trade Commission	

[a] All, except the GPO, are considered "designated federal entities" and placed directly under the 1978IG Act by the 1988 Amendments (P.L. 100-504) or subsequent enactments.

[b] In 1993, P.L. 103-82 merged ACTION into the new Corporation for National and Community Service.

[c] The Board for International Broadcasting was abolished by P.L. 103-236 and its functions and authorities transferred to the new International Broadcasting Bureau within USIA, which, in turn, was abolished and its functions transferred to the State Department.

[d] In 1993, P.L. 103-204 made the IG in FDIC a presidential appointee, subject to Senate confirmation.

[e] The FHLBB was abolished in 1989 by P.L. 101-73. The new FHFB was placed under the 1988 IG Act Amendments, also by P.L. 101-73.

[f] Unlike the designated federal entities, the GPO IG is not directly under the 1978 IG Act (P.L. 100-504).

[g] The ICC was abolished in1995 by P.L. 104-88.

[h] The Panama Canal Commission, replaced by the Panama Canal Commission Transition Authority, was phased out, when United States responsibility for the Canal was transferred to the Republic of Panama (22 U.S.C. 3611).

[i] P.L. 106-422 transferred TVA from a designated federal entity to a federal establishment.

[j] In 1996, the U.S. Postal Service Inspector General was separated from the Chief Postal Inspector and now exists as an independent position. The IG is appointed by, and can be removed by, the governors.

Table 4. Tabulation of Existing Federal Establishments, Entities, or Agencies with Statutory IGs

Controlling statute	IGs nominated by President and confirmed by Senate	IGs appointed by head of entity or agency	Total
1978 IG Act, as amended	28	27	55
Other statutes	1 [a]	1 [b]	2
Total	29	28	57

[a] CIA IG, P.L. 101-193.
[b] GPO IG, P.L. 100-504.

I. REPORTING, CONSULTATION, AND OTHER SOURCES OF INFORMATION

Congressional oversight of the executive is dependent to a large degree upon *information supplied by the agencies being overseen.* In the contemporary era, reporting and prior consultation provisions have increased in an attempt to ensure congressional access to Information, statistics, and other data on the workings of the executive. The result is that *approximately 4,000 reports arrive annually* on Capitol Hill. Concerns about unnecessary, duplicative, and wasteful reports, however, have prompted efforts to eliminate these. One such initiative, in part stimulated by earlier recommendations from the Vice President's National Performance Review and from the General Accounting Office, resulted in the Federal Reports Elimination and Sunset Acts of 1995 and 1998. Nonetheless, reductions in the number of required reports have not kept pace with new or continuing requirements, such as those identified in the 2001 Act to Prevent the Elimination of Certain Reports (P.L. 107-74).

1. Reporting Requirements

Reporting requirements affect executive and administrative agencies and officers, including the President; independent boards and commissions; and federally chartered corporations (as well as the judiciary). These statutory provisions vary in terms of the specificity, detail, and type of information that Congress demands. Reports may be required at periodic intervals, such as semiannually or at the end of a fiscal year, or submitted only if and when a specific event, activity, or set of conditions exists. The reports may also call upon an agency, commission, or officer to:

a. make a study and recommendations about a particular problem or concern;
b. alert Congress or particular committees and subcommittees in advance about a proposed or planned activity or operation;
c. provide information about specific ongoing or just-completed operations, projects, or programs; or
d. summarize an agency's activities for the year or the prior six months.

Examples of Reporting Requirements in Law

Initial Requirement in the 1789 Treasury Department Act:

"That it shall be the duty of the Secretary of the Treasury ... to make report, and give information to either branch of the legislature, in person or in writing (as he may be required), respecting all matters referred to him by the Senate or House of Representatives, or which shall appertain to his office ...." 1 Stat. 65-66 (1789)

Reporting on Covert Action in the 1991 Intelligence Oversight Act

"The President shall ensure that the intelligence committees are kept fully and currently informed of the intelligence activities of the United States, including any significant anticipated intelligence activity ...

(1) The President shall ensure that any finding [authorizing a covert action] shall be reported to the intelligence committees as soon as possible after such approval and before the initiation of the covert action, except as otherwise provided in paragraph (2) and paragraph (3).

(2) IF the President determines that it is essential to limit access to the finding to meet extraordinary circumstances affecting the vital interests of the United States, the finding may be reported to the chairmen and ranking minority members of the intelligence committees, the Speaker and minority leader of the House of Representatives, the majority and minority leaders of the Senate, and such other members of the congressional leadership as may be included by the President.

(3) Whenever a finding is not reported [in advance to the committees], the President shall fully inform the intelligence committees in a timely fashion and shall provide a statement of the reasons for not giving prior notice." 105 Stat. 441-443 (1991).

2. Prior Consultation

In the past, explicit prior consultation provisions were rarely incorporated into law. However, there appears to be an increase in statutory provisions as well as in committee reports that accompany legislation specifying conditions for such discussion (see box.)

A provision in the Conference committee report on the 1978 Ethics in Government Act illustrates this development: "The conferees expect the Attorney General to *consult* with the Judiciary Committees of both Houses of Congress *before* substantially the scope of authority or mandate of the Public Integrity Section of the Criminal Division."

3. Other Significant Sources of Information

A number of general management laws provide for additional sources of information, data, and material that can aid congressional oversight endeavors.

   a.   **Chief Financial Officers Act of 1990 (104 Stat. 2838).** The CFO act is designed to improve financial management throughout the federal government, through various procedures and mechanisms.

   1.   The act created two new posts within OMB, along with a new position of chief financial officer in 23 major federal agencies, including all Cabinet departments; a 24th agency has since been added.   Sixteen of these posts are filled by presidential appointees *subject to Senate confirmation*; these are in the 14 Cabinet departments plus the Environmental Protection Agency and the National Aeronautics and Space Administration.   The remaining eight CFO positions are in: the Agency for International Development, Federal Emergency Management Agency, General Services Administration, National Science Foundation, Nuclear Regulatory Commission, Office of Personnel Management, Small Business Administration, and the Social Security Administration.

   2.   The CFO act also provides for improvements in agency systems of accounting, financial management, and internal controls to assure the *issuance of reliable financial information* and to deter fraud, as well as waste and abuse of government resources.

   3.   The enactment, furthermore, calls for the production of *complete, reliable, timely, and consistent financial information for use by both the executive and the legislature* in the financing, management, and evaluation of federal programs.

   b.   **Government Performance and Results Act (107 Stat. 285).** This act – commonly known by the acronym GPRA or the Results Act – requires federal agencies to submit long-range strategic plans and follow-up annual performance plans.

   1.   Strategic Plans.   The strategic plans specify five-year goals and objectives for agencies, based on their basic missions and underlying statutory or other authority of the agency.   These plans, initially required in1997, were to be developed *in consultation with relevant congressional offices* and with information from "stakeholders" and then *submitted to Congress.*

   2.   Annual Performance Plans and Goals.   Based on these long-term plans, which may be modified if conditions and agency responsibilities change, the agencies are directed to set annual performance goals and to measure the results of their programs in achieving these goals. The objective of GPRA is to focus on *outcomes* – i.e., *the results and accomplishments of a program,* such as a decline in the use of illegal drugs for an anti-drug abuse program – rather than outputs, *i.e.* other measures of agency activity and operations, such as the number of anti-

drug agents in the field. The annual plans, which are also *available to Congress*, began with fiscal year 1999; the follow-up reports, which began in 2000, are required six months after the end of the fiscal year.

c. **Small Business Regulatory Enforcement Fairness Act of 1996 (110 Stat. 857-874).** Subtitle E of this act established, for the first time, a mechanism by which *Congress can review and disapprove virtually any federal rule or regulation.* It requires that:

1. All agencies promulgating a covered rule must submit a report *to each house of Congress and the Comptroller General,* containing specific information about the rule before it can go into effect.

2. Rules designated by the Office of Management and Budget as "major" may normally not go into effect *until 60 days after submission,* while non-major rules may become effective "as otherwise allowed in law," usually 30 days after publication in the *Federal Register.*

3. All covered rules are subject to *fast-track disapproval by passage of a joint resolution,* even if they have already gone into effect, for a period of at least 60 days. Upon enactment of such a joint resolution, no new rule that is "substantially the same" as the disapproved rule may be issued until it is *specifically authorized by a law* enacted subsequent to the disapproval of the original rule.

4. There can be no *judicial review of actions taken (or not taken) by Congress, the Comptroller General, or OMB*; but the failure of an agency to submit a covered rule for congressional review may be subject to sanction by a federal court.

d. **Paperwork Reduction Act of 1995 (109 Stat. 163).** This most recent version of paperwork reduction legislation builds on a heritage of statutory controls over government paperwork that dates to 1940.

1. Among other things, the current act and its 1980 predecessor more clearly defined the oversight responsibilities of OMB's Office of Information and Regulatory Affairs (OIRA); it is authorized to develop and administer uniform information policies in order to ensure *the availability and accuracy of agency data collection.*

2. Congressional oversight has been strengthened through its subsequent *reauthorizations* and the requirement for *Senate confirmation* of OIRA's administrator.

e. **Federal Managers' Financial Integrity Act (FMFIA) of 1982 (96 Stat. 814).** FMFIA is designed to improve the government's ability to manage its programs by strengthening internal management and financial controls, accounting systems, and financial reports.

1. The internal accounting systems are to be consistent with standards that the *Comptroller General* prescribes, including a requirement that all assets be safeguarded against waste, fraud, loss, unauthorized use, and misappropriation.

2. FMFIA also provides for *ongoing evaluations* of the internal control and accounting systems that protect federal programs against waste, fraud, abuse, and mismanagement.

3. The enactment further mandates that the head of each agency *report annually to the President and Congress* on the condition of these systems and on agency actions to correct any material weakness which the reports identify.

4. FMFIA is also connected to the Chief Financial Officers Act of 190, which calls upon the director of OMG to submit a financial management *status report to appropriate congressional committees;* part of this report is to be a summary of reports on internal accounting and administrative control systems as required by FMFIA.

f. **Cash Management Improvement act of 1990 (104 Stat. 1058).** This enactment is intended to *improve efficiency, effectiveness, and equity in the exchange of funds* between the federal government and state governments. Its fundamental objective is to prevent either level of government from engaging in cash management of practices that allow it to earn interest on cash reserves at the expense of the other.

g. **Information Technology Management Reform Act of 1996 (110 Stat. 679).** This act requires that agencies by the *best and most cost-effective information technology* available. To do so, the act gave more responsibility to individual agencies, revoking the primary role that the General Services Administration had played previously, and established the position of chief information officer (CIO) in federal agencies to provide relevant advise to agency heads.

J. RESOLUTIONS OF INQUIRY

Each chamber can call upon the executive for information through resolutions of inquiry.

1. These are usually *simple resolutions*, approved by only the House or Senate, rather than concurrent in form; they are never joint resolutions.

2. Resolutions of inquiry are addressed to either the President or heads of departments and agencies to supply specific factual information to the chamber. The resolutions usually *"request"* that the President or *"direct"* that administrative heads supply such information. In calling upon the President for information, especially about foreign affairs, the qualifying phrase – "if not incompatible with the public interest" – is usually added.

3. Such resolutions are to ask for facts, documents, or specific information; these devices are *not* to request an opinion or require an investigation (see box).

Resolution of Inquiry in Practice

The initial resolution of inquiry was approved on March 24, 1796, when the House sought documents in connection with the Jay Treaty negotiations:

> *Resolved,* That the President of the United States be requested to lay before this House a copy of the instructions to the minister of the United States, w ho negotiated the treaty with the Kind of Great Britain ... together with the correspondence and other documents relative to the said treaty; excepting such of the said papers as any existing negotiation may render improper to be delivered. (*Journal of the House of Representatives,* 4th Cong., 1st sess., March 24, 1796. p. 480.)

A contemporary illustration *occurred on March 1, 1995, when the House adopted H.Res.80, as amended (104th Cong. 1st sess),* 407-21. The resolution sought information about the Mexican peso crisis at the time and an Administration plan to use up to $20 billion in resources from the Exchange Stabilization Fund to help stabilize the Mexican currency and financial system. The resolution read:

> "*Resolved,* That the President, is hereby requested to provide the House of Representatives (consistent with the rules of the House), not later than 14 days after the adoption of this resolution, the following documents in the possession o f the executive branch, if not inconsistent with the public interest ..." The House request then specified the matters that the documents were to cover: The condition of the Mexican economy; consultations between the Government of Mexico, on the one hand, and the U.S. Secretary of the Treasury and/or the International Monetary fund, on the other; market policies and tax policies of the Mexican Government; and repayment agreements between Mexico and the United States; among other things.

K. Limitations and Riders on Appropriations

Congress uses a two-step legislative procedure: authorization of programs in bills reported by legislative committees followed by the financing of those programs in bills reported by the Committees on Appropriations. Congressional rules generally keep the two stages distinct and sequential. Authorizations should not be in general appropriations bills, nor appropriations in authorization measures. However, there are various exceptions to the general principle that congress should not make policy through the appropriations process. One exception is the practice of permitting "limitations" in an appropriations bill. "Riders" (language extraneous to the subject of the bill) are also added to control agency actions.

1. **Limitations.** Although House rules forbid in any general appropriations bill a provision "changing existing law," certain "limitations" may be admitted. "Just as the House under its rules may decline to appropriate for a purpose authorized by law, so it may be limitation prohibit the use of the money for part of the purpose while

appropriating for the remainder of it." Constitution, Jefferson's Manual, and Rules of the House of Representatives, H. Doc. No. 106-320, 106th Cong., 2d Sess. §1053 (2001). Limitations can be an effective device in oversight by strengthening Congress's ability to exercise control over federal spending and to reduce unnecessary or undesired expenditures. Under House Rule XXI, no provision changing existing law can be reported in any general appropriation bill "except germane provisions that retrench expenditures by the reduction of amounts of money covered by the bill" (the Holman rule). Rule XXI was amended in 1983 in an effort to restrict the number of limitations on appropriations bills. The rule was changed again in 1995 by granting the majority leader a central role in determining consideration of limitation amendments. The procedures for limitation in the House are set forth in the *Congressional Record* for January 6, 1999, p. H29. A well-known limitation is the Hyde amendment, which since the 1970s has restricted the use of Medicaid funds to fund abortions for indigent women (see box).

"None of the funds appropriated under this Act shall be expended for any abortion ... [except] (1) if the pregnancy is the result of an act of rape or incest; or (2) in the case where a woman suffers from a physical disorder, physical injury, or physical illness, including a life-endangering physical condition caused by or arising from the pregnancy itself, that would, as certified by a physician, place the woman in danger of death unless an abortion is performed." Labor-HHS Appropriations Act for fiscal 1998, 111 Stat. 1516, sec. 509 & 510 (1997).

---

2. **Riders.** Unlike limitations, legislative riders are extraneous to the subject matter of the bill to which they are added. Riders appear in both authorization bills and appropriations bills. In the latter, they may be subject to a point of order in the House on the ground that they are attempts to place legislation in an appropriations bill. In the Senate, Rule XVI prohibits on a point of order the addition to general appropriations bills of amendments that are legislative or nongermane. Both chambers have procedures to waive these prohibitions.

L. LEGISLATIVE VETO AND ADVANCE NOTICE

Many acts of Congress have delegated authority to the executive branch on the condition that proposed actions be submitted to Congress for review and possible disapproval before they can be put into effect. This way of ensuring continuing oversight of policy areas follows two paths: the legislative veto and advance notification.

1. Legislative Veto

Beginning in 1932, Congress delegated authority to the executive branch with the condition that proposed executive actions would be first submitted to congress and subjected to disapproval by either house or disapproval by both houses acting through a concurrent resolution. Over the years, other types of legislative veto were added, allowing Congress to control executive branch actions without having to enact a law. In 1983, the Supreme Court ruled that the legislative veto was unconditional on the ground that all exercises of legislative power that affect the right, duties, and relations of persons outside the legislative branch must satisfy the constitutional requirements of bicameralism and presentment of a bill or resolution to the President for his signature or veto. *INS v. Chadha*, 462 U.S. 919 (1983). Despite this ruling, Congress has continued to enact proscribed legislative vetoes and it has also relied on informal arrangements to provide comparable controls.

a. Legislative Vetoes in Statute

Congress responded to *Chadha* by converting some of the one-house and two-House legislative vetoes to joint resolutions of approval or disapproval, thus satisfying the requirements of bicameralism and presentment. However, Congress continues to rely on legislative vetoes. Since the *Chadha* decision, more than 400 legislative vetoes have been enacted into public law, usually in appropriations acts. These legislative vetoes are exercised by the Appropriations Committees. Typically, funds may not be used or an executive action may not begin until the Appropriations Committees. Typically, funds may not be used or an executive action may not begin until the Appropriations Committees have approved or, at least, not disapproved the planned action, often within a specified time limit (see box).

For the appropriation account "Transportation Administrative Service Center." No assessments may be levied against any program, budget activity, subactivity or project funded by this statute "unless notice of such assessments and the basis therefore are presented to the House and Senate Committees on Appropriations and are approved by such Committees." Department of Transportation and Related Agencies Appropriations Act 2001, 114 Stat. 1356A-2 (2000).

---

b. Informal Legislative Vetoes

Unlike a formal legislative veto, where the arrangement is spelled out in the law, the informal legislative veto occurs where an executive official pledges not to proceed with an activity until Congress or certain committees agree to it. An example of this appeared during the 101st Congress; in the "bipartisan accord" on funding the contras in Nicaragua, the Administration pledged that no funds would be obligated beyond November 30, 1989, unless affirmed by letter from the relevant authorizations committees and the bipartisan leadership of Congress.

2. Advance Notification or Report-and-Wait

Statutory provisions may stipulate that before a particular activity can be undertaken by the executive branch or funds obligated, Congress must first be advised or informed, ordinarily through a full written statement, of what is being proposed. These statutory provisions usually provide for a period of time during which action by the executive must be deferred, giving Congress an opportunity to pass legislation prohibiting the pending action or using political pressure to cause executive officials to retract or modify the proposed action. This type of "report and wait" provision has been upheld by the Supreme Court. The Court noted: "The value of the reservation of the power to examine proposed rules, laws and regulations before they become effective is well understood by Congress. It is frequently, as here, employed to make sure that the action under the delegation squares with the Congressional purpose." *Sibbach v. Wilson*, 312 U.S. 1 (1941). An example appeared in the Comprehensive Anti-Apartheid Act of 1986, which was directed toward South Africa's political persecution of Nelson Mandela and other dissidents (see box).

"The President may suspend or modify any of the measures required by this title or section 501(c) or section 504(b) thirty days after he determines, and so reports to the Speaker of the House of Representatives and the chairman of the Committee on Foreign Relations of the Senate, that the Government of South Africa has [taken certain actions] unless the Congress enacts within such 30-day period, in accordance with section 602 of this Act, a joint resolution disapproving the determination of the President under this subsection." 100 Stat.

M. INDEPENDENT COUNSEL

The statutory provisions for the appointment of an independent counsel (formerly called "special prosecutor") were originally enacted as Title VI of the Ethics in Government Act of 1978, and codified at 28 U.S.C. §§ 591-599. The independent counsel was reauthorized in 1983, 1987, and 1994. It expired on June 30, 1999. The mechanisms of the independent counsel law were triggered by the receipt of information by the attorney general that alleged a violations of any federal criminal law (other than certain misdemeanors or "infractions") by a person covered by the act. Certain high-level federal officials, including the President, Vice President, and heads of departments, were automatically covered by the law. In addition, the Attorney General had discretion to seek an independent counsel for any person for whom there may exist a personal, financial or political conflict of interest for Justice Department personnel to investigate; and the attorney general could seek an independent counsel for any Member of Congress when the attorney general deemed it to be in the "public interest."

After conducting a limited review of the matter (a 30-day threshold review of the credibility and specificity of the charges, and a subsequent 90-day preliminary investigation, with a possible 60-day extension) the Attorney General, if he or she believed that "further investigation is warranted", would apply to a special "division of the court," a federal three-judge panel appointed by the Chief Justice of the Supreme Court, requesting that the division appoint an independent counsel. The Attorney General of the United States was the *only* officer in the government authorized to apply for the appointment of an independent counsel.

The special division of the court, and designated his or her prosecutorial jurisdiction, based on the information provided the court by the Attorney General. The independent counsel had the full range of investigatory and prosecutorial powers and functions of the attorney general or other Department of justice employees.

There was no specific term of appointment for independent counsels. They could serve for as long as it took to complete their duties concerning that specific matter within their defined and limited jurisdiction. One a matter was completed, the independent counsel filed a final report. The special division of the court could also find that the independent counsel's work was completed and terminate the office. A periodic review of an independent counsel for such determination was to be made by the special division of the court. An independent counsel, *prior* to the completion of his or her duties, could be removed form office (other than by impeachment and conviction) only by the attorney general of the United States for good cause, physical or mental disability, or other impairing condition, and such removal could be appealed to the court. The procedures for appointing and removing the independent counsel were upheld by the Supreme Court in *Morrison v. Olson*, 487 U.S. 654 (1988).

Collisions between Congress and Independent Counsels

"The Congress' role here is terribly important. It is for them to present to the public as soon as possible a picture of the actual facts as to the Iran/Contra matters. This is so because there has been so much exposed without sufficient clarity to clear up the questions. There is a general apprehension that this is damaging. Congress properly wants to bring this to an end soon and that gives them a real feeling of urgency for their investigation.

"[The House and Senate Iran-Contra Committees] are trying to provide a factual predicate which will enable Congress to decide intelligently whether there is a need for a statutory amendment or for a closer oversight over covert activities and other matters ... As they quite properly point out, they cannot wait for independent Counsel to satisfy himself as to whether a crime may or may not have been committed. They have a problem of their own.

"... We are proceeding with much greater detail than Congress would think necessary for their purposes. We come into collision when the question of immunity arises.

"... There is a greater pressure on Congress to grant immunity to central figures than there is for Independent Counsel. Over the last three months, we have had long negotiations over this question of immunity ...

"If the Congress decides to grant immunity, there is no way that it can be avoided. They have the last word and that is a proper distribution of power.....

"...The reason why Congress must have this power to confer immunity is because of the importance of their role. The legislative branch has the power to decide whether it is more important perhaps even to destroy a prosecution than to hold back testimony they need."

Lawrence E. Walsh, "The Independent Counsel and the Separation of Powers," Houston Law Review, v. 25 (1988):1.

Investigation by the independent counsel could compete with parallel efforts by congressional committees to examine the same issue. Congress could decide to accommodate the needs of the independent counsel, such as delaying a legislative investigation until the independent counsel completed certain phases of an inquiry (see box on previous page).

Although Congress could call on the Attorney General to apply for an independent counsel by a written request from the House or Senate Judiciary Committee, or a majority of members of either party of those committees, the Attorney General is not required to begin a preliminary investigation or to apply for an independent counsel in response to such a request. However, in such cases the Justice Department was required to provide certain information to the requesting committee.

The independent counsel was directed by statutory language to submit to Congress an annual report on the activities of such independent counsel, including the progress of investigations and any prosecutions. Although it was recognized that certain information would have to be kept confidential, the statute stated that "information adequate to justify the expenditures that the office of the independent counsel has made" should be provided. 28 U.S.C. §595(a)(2).

The conduct of an independent counsel was subject to congressional oversight and an independent counsel was required to cooperate with that oversight. 28 U.S.C. §595(a)(1). In addition, the independent counsel was required to report to the House of Representatives any 'substantial and credible" information that may constitute grounds for any impeachment. 28 U.S.C. §595(c). On September 11, 1998, Independent Counsel Kenneth W. Starr forwarded to the House a report concluding that President Clinton may have committed impeachable offenses. The House passed two articles of impeachment (perjury and obstruction of justice), but the Senate voted only 45 to 55 on the perjury charge and 50 to 50 on the obstruction of justice charge, both votes short of the two-thirds majority required under the Constitution.

The independent counsel statute expired in 1992, partly because of criticism directed at Lawrence Walsh's investigation of Iran-Contra. The statute was reauthorized in 1994, but objections to the investigations conducted by Kenneth Starr against Whitewater, Monica Lewinsky, and other matters, put Congress under pressure to let the statute lapse on June 30, 1999.

Unless Congress in the future reauthorizes the independent counsel, the only available option for an independent counsel is to have the Attorney General invoke existing authority to appoint a special prosecutor to investigate a particular matter. For example, when the independent counsel statute expired in 1992 and was not reauthorized until 1994, Attorney General Janet Reno appointed Robert Fiske in 1993 to investigate the Clintons' involvement in Whitewater and the death of White House aide Vincent Foster. On July 9, 1999 Attorney General Reno promulgated regulations concerning the appointment of outside, temporary counsels, to be called "Special Counsels," in certain circumstances to conduct investigations and possible prosecutions of certain sensitive matters, or matters which may raise a conflict for the Justice Department (28 D.F.R. Part 600). Such special counsels will have substantially less independence than the statutory independent General, including removal for "misconduct, dereliction of duty, incapacity, conflict of interest, or for other good cause, including violation of Department policies."

SELECTED READINGS

Statutory Offices of Inspector General

Hendricks, Michael, et al. Inspectors General: A New Force in Evaluation. San Francisco: Jossey-Bass, Inc, 1990.

Kaiser, Frederick M. Statutory Office of Inspector General: Establishment and Evolution. CRS Report 98-379 GOV, August 10, 2001.

_____. "The Watchers' Watchdog: The CIA Inspector General." International Journal of Intelligence and Counterintelligence, v. 3, 1989, pp. 55-75.

_____ and Diane T. Duffy. Statutory Offices of Inspector General: A 205h Anniversary Review. CRS Report 98-141 GOV, November 20, 1998.

Light, Pal C. Monitoring Government: Inspectors General and the Search for Accountability. Washington: Brookings, 1993.

HJ9801.L54

Newcomer, Kathryn E. The Changing Nature of Accountability: The Role of the Inspectors General in Federal Agencies. Public Administration Review, vol. 58, March/April, 1998.

U.S. Congress. House Committee on Government Operations. The Inspector General Act of 1978: A Ten-Year Review. Washington: GPO, 1988.

U.S. Congress. House Committee on Government Reform and Oversight. Subcommittee on Government Management, Information, and Technology. The Inspector General Act of 1978: Twenty Years After Passage, Are the Inspectors General Fulfilling Their Mission. Hearings, 105th Congress, 2d Session, Washington: G.P.O., 1998, and Inspector General Act Oversight, Hearings, 103rd Congress, 2d Session. Washington: GPO, 1996.

U.S. Congress. Senate Committee on Governmental Affairs. The Inspector General Act: 20 Years Later. Hearings, 105th Congress, 2d Session. Washington: G.P.O., 1998.

Reporting, Consultation, and Other Sources of Information

Collier, Ellen C. "Reporting Requirements." In Joint Committee on the Organization of Congress. Congressional Reorganization: Proposals for Change. Senate Print 103-19, 103d Cong., 1st sess. Washington: GPO, 1993. p. 135.

_____. "Foreign Policy by Reporting Requirement." The Washington Quarterly, vol. 11, Winter 1988.

Government Performance and Results Act: Implementing the Results. CRS Info Pack IP 517G, 1999.

Johannes, John. "Statutory Reporting Requirements: Information and Influence for Congress." In Abdo Baaklini, ed., Comparative Legislative Reforms and Innovations. New York: SUNY Press, 1977. pp. 33-60.

Moe, Ronald C., project coordinator. General Management Laws: A Selective Compendium. CRS Report RL30895, January 8, 2001.

Rosenberg, Morton. Congressional Review of agency Rulemaking: A Brief Overview and Assessment After Five Years. CRS Report RL 30116, March 6, 2001.

_____. "Whatever Happened to Congressional Review of Agency Rulemaking?: A Brief Overview, Assessment, and Proposal for Reform. Administrative Law Review, vol. 51, No. 4. Fall 1999: 1051-1092.

U.S. General Accounting Office. Investigators' Guide to Sources of Information. GAO Report OSI-9702. Washington: GAO, 1997.

US. General Accounting Office. A Systematic Management Approach Is Needed for Congressional Reporting Requirements. GAO Report PAD-82-12. Washington: GAO, 1981.

U.S. House of Representatives. Clerk. Reports To Be Made to Congress. Hose Document 106-37, 106th Congress, 1st session. Washington: GPO, 1999.

U.S. House of Representatives. Committee on Government Reform and oversight. Laws Related to Federal Financial Management. .House Report 104-745, 104th Congress, 2nd Session. Washington: GPO, 1996.

U.S. Vice President Al Gore. National Performance Review. Crating a Government that Works Better & Costs Less: Streamlining Management Control. Washington: Office of the Vice President, 1993 (Reduce the Burden of Congressionally Mandated Reports, pp. 33-36).

Resolutions of Inquiry

Beth, Richard. Resolutions of Inquiry in the House of Representatives: A Brief Description. CRS Report 87-365 GOV, April 22, 1987.

History of the United States House of Representatives, 1789-1994, H. Doc. 103-324, 103d Cong., 2d sess. Washington: GPO, 1994 (Resolutions of Inquiry, pp. 260-262).

Methods and Techniques

Art, Robert J. "Congress and the Defense Budget: Enhancing Policy Oversight," Political Science Quarterly, v. 100, Summer 1985: 227-248.

Bowers, James R. Regulating the Regulators: An Introduction to the Legislative Oversight of Administrative Rulemaking. New York: Praeger, 1990. 140p.

KF5411.B69

Hill, James P. "The Third House of Congress Versus the Fourth Branch of Government: The Impact of Congressional Committee Staff on Agency Regulatory Decision-Making," John Marshall Law Review, v. 19, Winer 1986: 247-273.

Kaiser, Frederick M. "Congressional Oversight of the Presidency," Annals of the American Academy of Political and Social Science, v. 499, Sept. 1988: 75-89.

U.S. Congress. Senate. Committee on Government Operations [now titled governmental Affairs]. Subcommittee on Oversight Procedures. Committee Print. Congressional Oversight: Methods and Techniques. 94th Congress, 2d Session, July 1976. Washington: G.P.O., 1976. 254p.

Special Studies and Investigations by Staff and Others

Johannes, John R. To Serve the People: Congress and Constituency Service. Lincoln, University of Nebraska Press, 1984.

JK1071.J63

Kaiser, Frederick M. A Congressional Office of Constituent Assistance: Proposals, Rationales, and Possible Objections. CRS Report 91-893 GOV, December 18, 1991.

Pontius, John S. and George Walser. Casework in a Congressional Office. CRS Report No. 98-878, July 12, 2001.

The Press and Media

Coo, Timothy E. Making Laws and Making news. Washington. The Brookings Institution, 1989. 210p.

JK1447.C66

Graber, Doris A. Mass Media and American Politics, 6th ed. Washington: CQ Press, 2001.

HN90.M3G7

Hess, Stephen. Live from Capitol Hill. Washington: The Brookings Institution, 1991. 178 p.

PN4888.P6H48

Mann, Thomas and Norman Ornstein, eds. Congress, the Press, and the Public. Washington: The American Enterprise Institute and The Brookings Institution, 1994. 212 p.

JK1140.C62

Ritchie, Donald A. Press Gallery: Congress and the Washington Correspondents. Cambridge, Mass.: Harvard University Press, 1991.

PN4899.W3R58

Specialized Investigations

Congressional Quarterly. Guide to Congress. Washington: Congressional Quarterly, Inc., 2000, 5th ed. Vol. I, pp. 249-280.

Dimock, Marshall E. Congressional Investigating Committees. Baltimore: Johns Hopkins Press, 1929.

KF4942.D5

Eberling, Ernest J. Congressional Investigations. New York: Columbia University Press, 1929.

JK1123.A2E2

Fisher, Louis. Constitutional Conflicts between Congress and the President. Lawrence, Kansas: University Press of Kansas, 1997, 4th revised ed. Pp. 160-195.

KF4565.F57

_____. Congressional Access to Executive Branch Information: Legislative Tools. CRS Report No. RL30966, May 17, 2001.

Hamilton, James. The Power to Probe: A Study of Congressional Investigations. New York: Vintage Books, 1976.

KF4942.H34

Kaiser, Frederick M. "Impact and Implications of the Iran-contra Affair on Congressional Oversight of the Executive." International Journal of Intelligence and Counterintelligence, vol. 7, Summer 1994, pp. 205-234.

Mayhew, David R. Divided We Govern: Party Control, Lawmaking, and Investigations, 1946-1990. New Haven: Yale University Press, 1991.

JK2261.M36

Schlesinger, Arthur M. Jr. and Roger Bruns. Congress Investigates: A Documented History. New York: Chelsea House, 1975 (5 vols.).

JK1123.A2S34

Taylor, Telford. The Grand Inquest: The Story of Congressional Investigations New York: Simon and Schuster, 1955.

KF4942.T38

Appropriations Limitations and Riders

Banks, William C. and Peter Raven-Hanse. National Security Law and the Power of the Purse. New York, Oxford University Press, 1994. 260 p.

KF4651.B36

Devins, Neal. "Regulation of Government Agencies Through Limitation Riders," Duke Law Journal, v. 1987: 456.

Fisher, Louis. 'The Authorization-Appropriation Process in Congress; Formal Rules and Informal Practices," Catholic University Law Review, v. 29, 1979:5.

Keith, Robert. "Legislative Provisions ('Riders') in Omnibus Appropriations Acts: Recent Examples." CRS Report 98-834 GOV, October 28, 1998.

LeBoeuf, Jacques B. "Limitations on the Use of Appropriations Riders by Congress to Effectuate Substantive Policy Changes," Hastings Constitutional law Quarterly, v. 19, 1992: 457.

The Legislative Veto

Biden, Joseph R., Jr. "Who Needs the Legislative Veto?" Syracuse Law Review, v. 35, 1984: 685.

Breyer, Stephen. "The Legislative Veto After *Chadha*." Georgetown Law Journal, v. 72, 1984: 785.

Craig, Barbara Hinson. Chadha: The Story of an Epic Constitutional Struggle. New York: Oxford University Press, 1988.

KF228.C43C73

Fisher, Louis. "The Legislative Veto: Invalidated, It Survives," Law & Contemporary Problems. V. 56, 1993: 273.

Gibson, Martha Liebler. Weapons of Influence: the Legislative Veto, American Foreign Policy, and the Irony of Reform. Boulder, Colo., Westview Press, 1992. 188 p.

JX1706.G53

Kaiser, Frederick M. "Congressional Action to Overturn Agency Rules: Alternatives to the 'legislative veto.'" Administrative Law Review, v. 32, 1980: 667.

Korn, Jessica. The Power of Separation: American Constitutionalism and the Myth of the Legislative Veto. Princeton, N.J.: Princeton University Press, 1996. 178 p.

JK305.K67

Independent Counsel

Eastland, Terry. Ethics, Politics and the independent counsel. Washington, National Legal Center for the public Interest, 1989. 180 p.

KF4568.E17 1989

Harriger, Katy J. The Special Prosecutor in American Politics, 2d ed. Revised. Lawrence, University Press of Kansas, 2000. 325 p.

KF4568.H37

Jost, Kenneth. "Independent Counsels: Should Congress make major changes in the law?" CQ Researcher, v. 7, no. 7, February 21, 1997: 145-167.

Koukoutchos, Brian Stuart. Constitutional Kinetics: The Independent counsel Case and the Separation of Powers. Wake Forest law review, v. 23, 1988: 635.

Maskell, Jack. The Independent Counsel Law. The Federal Lawyer, July 1998: 28-39.

Nolan, Beth. "Removing Conflicts from the Administration of justice: Conflicts of Interest and Independent Counsels Under the Ethics in Government Act." Georgetown Law Journal, v. 79, 1990: 1-80.

Walsh, Lawrence E. The Independent Counsel and the Separation of Powers. Houston Law Review, v. 25, 1988: 1.

V. Oversight Information Sources and Consultant Services

Congress calls upon a variety of sources for information and analysis to support its oversight activities. Most of this assistance is provided by legislative support agencies: Congressional Research Service, the Congressional Budget Office, and the General Accounting Office. In addition, the Offices of Senate Legal Counsel and House General Counsel are valuable oversight resources. A range of outside interest groups and research organizations also provide rich sources of information.

A. Congressional Research Service (CRS)

1. CRS Mission Statement

"The Congressional Research Service provides the Congress, throughout the legislative process, comprehensive and reliable legislative research, analysis, and information services that are timely, objective, nonpartisan, and confidential, thereby contributing to an informed national legislature."

2. Organization

CRS is organized into six research divisions and five specialized offices. The research divisions are American Law; Domestic Social Policy; Foreign Affairs, Defense and Trade; Government and Finance; Information Research; and Resources, Science, and Industry.

3. Staff on CRS

CRS has 700 authorized full-time equivalents (FTEs) on its permanent staff. The professional staff are diverse, including, among others, attorneys, economists, engineers, social science analysts, information scientists, librarians, defense and foreign affairs analysts, political scientists, public administrators, and physical, biological, and behavioral scientists.

The highest level researchers are senior specialists, who have national and international recognition in their fields.

4. CRS Work for Congress

CRS provides the following services:

Analytical and Research Services

a. Policy Analysis and Research

CRS staff anticipates and responds to congressional needs for policy analysis and information in an interdisciplinary, integrated manner. CRS provides timely and objective responses to congressional inquiries for policy analysis and information at every stage of the legislative process.

Legislative attorneys and paralegal staff respond to congressional needs for legal information and analysis to support the legislative, oversight, and representational functions of Congress.

b. Information Research

Expert information research specialists and resource specialists are available to provide information research and reference assistance. The staff also provides copies of articles in newspapers, journals, legal and legislative documents and offers assistance with a wide variety of electronic files.

c. Briefings, Seminars, and Workshops

CRS conducts briefings, seminars, and workshops for Members of Congress and their staff. On these occasions CRS analysts and other experts discuss public policy issues, international concerns, and the legislative process.

Briefings. CRS analysts and specialists are available to give one-on-one briefings to Members and staff on public policy issues, the legislative process, congressional office operations, committee mattes, or general orientation to CRS.

Issue seminars and workshops. In anticipation of congressional interest or at the request of a Member or Committee, CRS organizes and conducts seminars and workshops on issues of current interest to Members and staff of Congress. CRS and outside experts participate in these events with Members and staff.

Federal Law Update. This series, offered twice yearly by the American Law Division, focuses on developments in federal law and issues before the Supreme Court. The series can meet continuing legal education (CLE) requirements in some states.

CRS Legislative Institutes. This three-part series provides training in the work of Congress and the legislative process. Topics include the federal budget process, committee system and procedures, floor procedures, amendments, and resolutions. IN the Graduate

Legislative Institute, participants simulate congressional proceedings as "members of the CRS Congress" and gain experience in procedures by moving bills through the legislative process.

Public Policy Issues Institute. Held at the beginning of each session of the Congress, this program provides introductory briefings and discussions by CRS staff on issues of legislative significance to the Congress.

District and Staff Institutes. These institutes provide orientation for staff of district offices that include discussions of CRS services, the legislative and budget processes, casework, Member allowances, ethics, and franking. The program is supported by the House and Senate.

New Member Seminar. Every two years CRS offers new Members an orientation seminar on public policy issues. These sessions are held in January at the beginning of each new Congress.

For additional information about CRS seminars and evens, call 7-7904.

Written Products

a. Customized Memoranda

Confidential memoranda prepared for a specific office are a major form of CRS written communication. These memoranda are solely for the use of the requesting office and are not distributed further unless permission has been given by that office. Memoranda are often used by CRS attorneys and analysts to respond to inquiries focused on legislative and policy matters of individual Member interest.

b. CRS Reports for Congress

Reports for Congress on specific issues take many forms: policy analyses, statistical reviews, economic studies, legal analyses, historical studies, chronological reviews, and bibliographies. Short CRS Reports – six pages or fewer – are available for direct delivery on Capitol Hill to the requester's fax machine via the CRS Fax-on Demand service at 7-9943. Reports are available on the CRS Web site (www.loc.gov/crs).

c. Issue Briefs

CRS prepares concise briefing pages on issues before the Congress. Updated regularly, Issue Briefs are available both in printed form and on the CRS Web site.

d. General Distribution Memoranda

Matters that are not suitable for treatment in a CRS Report or Issue Brief, but that may be of interest to more than one congressional office, can be the subject of general distribution memoranda provided to a congressional office upon request. The memoranda differ from Reports because they are tailored, or written for a single requester; are directed to a specific question or concern; or are more technical or focused in nature.

e. Info Packs

Info Packs are compilations of materials on issues before Congress and provide background information on a particular topic. Most include Reports as well as other CRS products. They are also useful in responding to constituent requests. A complete collection of Info Packs is available for walk-in service in the Senate Research Center in room SR-B07 of the Russell Building and the Product Distribution Center in room LM-212 of the James Madison Memorial Building; selected Info Packs are provided at all CRS Reference Centers.

f. CRS Research Centers

In the three CRS Research Centers in congressional office buildings, reference librarians assist with telephone and in-person inquiries. Each center provides access to reference collections and CRS products.

Longworth Research Center
Rayburn Research Center
Russell Senate Research Center
Hours: Monday-Friday, 9:00 a.m.-6:00 p.m.
(Hours may change when Congress is not in session.)

g. Electronically Accessible Products and Services

CRS Web Site (http://www.loc.gov/crs): The CRS Web site provides 24-hour access to an array of CRS services including full test of issue briefs and reports, a weekly "Legislative Alert," updates and analyses of the annual appropriations legislation, an interactive guide to the legislative process, online registration for CRS seminars, and complete information on other CRS services. The CRS Web site also offers links to a selection of other Internet sites providing public policy, legislative, legal, and quick reference information. In operation since the 104th Congress, the CRS Web site is accessible only to House and Senate offices and other legislative branch agencies. The Service recently added Electronic Briefing Books, bill summary and status information, extensive coverage of all appropriations legislation, weekly alerts to CRS products related to floor action, and public policy literature abstracts. A linked format allows the user to move easily within the online document, link to the text and summary of relevant legislation, and link to other CRS products on the topic as well as to sources of information outside CRS.

Legislative Information System (http://www.congress.gov): At the beginning of the 105th Congress, a new Legislative Information System (LIS) was available for the first time on the Cap NET component of Internet. The system provides Members of Congress and their staff with access to the most current and comprehensive legislative information available. It can be accessed only by the House and Senate and the legislative support agencies. The LIS is being developed under the policy direction of the Senate Committee on Rules and Administration and the House Administration Committee. It is a collaborative project of the offices and agencies of the legislative branch, including the secretary of the Senate and the clerk of the House; House Information Resources; the Senate Computer Center; the Senate Office of Telecommunications; the Government Printing Office; the General Accounting

Office; the Congressional Budget Office; the Congressional Research Service; and the Library of Congress.

CRS has responsibility for the overall coordination of development of retrieval system; the Library of Congress is responsible for its technical development and operation. The Service recently developed links from CRS products and services listed on LIS to relevant congressional documents and began to develop more efficient linkages and sharing of legislative information among the three branches of government as well as with nongovernmental sources.

Legislative Alert: The Legislative Alert, a weekly compendium of CRS products relevant to scheduled or expected floor action, is available by fax and e-mail subscription to all Members, committees, and subcommittees. Full text of all CRS products listed on the Alert is accessible electronically on the CRS Web site.

Optical Disk: Congressional staff can use special optical disk work stations located in CRS reading rooms and reference centers to identify, view, and print the full text of CRS products and articles form the Public Policy Literature file (PPLT).

Fax-on-Demand: The CRS Fax-on-Demand system enables congressional and committee offices on Capitol Hill to have selected CRS products faxed directly to them. The system contains full text of all active short CRS reports (those with six or fewer pages) written since January 1993, the weekly update, and invitations to seminars.

SCORPIO: CRS and the Library of Congress maintain a computer-based information retrieval system called SCORPIO. It can be searched by congressional staff from terminals located in CRS readings rooms and reference centers, in the Library of Congress, and in most congressional offices. The system is comprised of data bases containing information on legislation, public policy literature, CRS products, bill digests, public opinion polls, books, serials, maps, and other materials available in the Library. Staff can search SCORPIO data bases through any easy-to-use screen interface, known as ACCESS, in CRS reading rooms and reference centers.

h. Economic Statistics: StatsLine

The CRS StatsLine provides a recorded message, updated weekly, on selected economic indicators: the consumer price index, federal deficit, gross national product housing starts, the prime rate, public debt, unemployment, and the US. merchandise trade balance. To reach the StatsLine, call 7-7034.

i. Audiovisual Products and Services

CRS produces a variety of video and audio cassette programs on public policy issues as well as on legislative procedures. The programs, which range from 30 to 60 minutes, feature CRS analysts and other national experts. Television programs on topics of current interest are shown each weekday on congressional channel 5 in the Senate and channel 6 in the House at 12:00 noon and at 4:00 p.m.

5. CRS Divisional Responsibilities

CRS analysts and information research specialists provide assistance in response to requests from Members and committees of Congress at all stages of the legislative process. The Service uses an interdisciplinary and integrative approach as it addresses questions that emerge from program and policy issues on the congressional agenda as well as from the representative and oversight roles of the Congress. CRS seeks to define complex issues in clear and understandable ways, identify basic causes of the problems under consideration, and highlight available policy choices and potential effects of actions. The Service is organized into the following divisions and offices to support the analysis, research, and information needs of the Congress.

Divisions

The American Law Division responds to congressional requests for legal analysis and information involving federal and state statutory and case law. The division's work spans the range of legal questions from constitutional questions of separate of powers and legislative-executive relations to inquiries arising out of federal, state, and international law. Analysis of litigation affecting the work of Congress and the congressional response to judicial developments also forms the basis of much of the division's work. Staff have expertise in fields such as constitutional law, congressional ethics, civil rights law, environmental law, criminal law, administrative law, and congressional practices and procedures. In addition, the division prepared *The Constitution of the United States of America – Analysis and Interpretation* (popularly known as the *Constitution Annotated*).

The Domestic Social Policy Division works closely with the Congress to provide analysis and research on domestic policy and social program issues. Analysts use an interdisciplinary approach to integrate program analysis, education and training; labor and occupational safety; health care and medicine; Social Security; welfare, nutrition, and housing; public and private pensions; unemployment compensation and worker's compensation; immigration; civil rights; crime and criminal justice; and issues and programs related to children, persons with disabilities, the aged, the poor, veterans, and minorities.

The Foreign Affairs, Defense, and Trade Division is organized into regional and functional sections. Analysts follow worldwide political and economic developments including U.S. relations with individual counties and transnational issues such as terrorism, refugees, global economic problems, and global institutions such as the International Monetary Fund and the World Trade Organization. They also address U.S. foreign aid programs, strategies, and resource allocations; State Department budget and functions; international debt; public diplomacy; and legislation on foreign relations. Other work includes national security policy, military strategy, weapons systems, military compensation, the defense budget, and U.S. military bases. Trade-related legislation, policies, and programs and U.S. trade performance and investment flows are covered, as are trade negotiations and agreements, export promotion, import regulations, tariffs, and trade policy functions.

The Government and Finance Division responds to congressional requests for assistance on all aspects of the Congress: its congressional budget and appropriations process; its legislative process; legislative branch agencies; and executive-legislative relations. In addition the division responds to requests on the organization and management of the executive branch; the Presidency and Vice Presidency; intergovernmental relations and state and local governments; District of Columbia; statehood and territories; rural and urban development; small business and economic development; federal statistical policy; survey research and public opinion polls; census, reapportionment, and redistricting; elections, lobbying, and political parties; U.S. and constitutional history; information policy and privacy; banking, insurance, and securities, macroeconomic policy analysis; fiscal and monetary policy; taxation; and government finance.

The **Information Research Division** responds to requests for information research and reference assistance. Staff use written reports, standard reference works, automated research tools, the Internet, and a variety of collections both in the Library and elsewhere to locate information on people, organizations, events, and public policy issues. Information is prepared in a number of different formats, including written reports, tailored packets, Info Packs, and electronic files easily available through the CRS Web site. The staff in the reading rooms and research centers provide telephone reference service and in-person consultation on resources available for research projects. The Product Distribution Center provides document deliver service for CRS products.

The **Resources, Science, and Industry Division** covers an array of legislative issues involving natural resources and environmental management; science and technology; and industry infrastructure. Resources work includes policy analyses on public lands, natural resources, environmental, agriculture, food, fisheries, energy, and mineral issues. Science coverage includes policy analysis on civilian and military research and development issues; information and telecommunications; space; earth sciences; and general science and technology. Support on industry issues includes policy analysis on transportation and transportation infrastructure issues; industrial market structure and regulation; and sector-specific industry analysis.

Offices

The **Office of Finance and Administration** maintains oversight of the financial and administrative activities of the Service; exercise responsibility for planning and directing the fiscal operations of the Service, including development of annual strategic performance plans, appropriation requests and related budget estimates, budget execution, external contracting, fundraising, and procurement; and represents the Director in handling issues involving the Service's status, role, activities, and interacting with other Library entities in relevant areas of planning, management, budget, and administration.

The **Office of Information Resources Management** develops and maintains information services that support both the congress and CRS staff. These services include the congressional legislative information retrieval system (LIS), which provides access to a wide variety of products produced by CRS and other government sources, and the Bill Digest, an on-line legislative documentation database for the Congress that analyzes, summarizes, and tracks the status of congressional legislation. The office provides information support to CRS staff through its provision of library management, reference service, procurement of electronic and print resources, training in the use of electronic resources, and Intranet resource development.

The Office of Policy and Quality Assurance, through the Office of Review, the Office of Policy Implementation, and the Electronic Research Products Office, plans, develops, and coordinates matters relating to internal CRS policies, particularly as they affect the Service's relationships with congressional clients and other legislative support agencies; provides final CRS review and clearance of all CRS products; ensures that the Service complies with applicable guidelines and directives contained in the Legislative Reorganization Act, in statements by appropriations and oversight committees and in Library regulations and CRS policy statements; and edits, produces, and distributes electronic CRS documents.

The Office of Research Operations provides operational support to facilitate CRS research performed for the Congress. Within the Office, the Legislative Relations Office receives and assigns congressional inquiries to the research divisions, works with the divisions to plan and carry out institutes, seminars, and briefings for Members, committees, and congressional staff; and examines and strengthens the Service's outreach to congressional leadership and Member and committee offices. The Management Information Office within Research Operations records and tracks data on congressional inquiries and CRS responses. This office also develops and refines systems designed to provide managers with statistical information needed to analyze subject coverage, client service, and the use of resources. The Technology Office builds and maintains the technology infrastructure of the Service as a whole, develops and applies new technologies to enhance CRS productivity, and develops applications for communication of CRS research to its clients.

The Office of Work Force Development administers the Service's workforce development programs, including succession planning, special recruitment programs, merit selection and other employment programs, mentoring, diversity efforts, special recognition programs, upward mobility programs, training, and position and performance management programs and activities. It represents the Director in issues involving the Service's status, role, activities, and interaction with other Library entities in relevant areas of human resources management and administration.

6. **Interdisciplinary Teams**

a. **Identification of Major Issues**

As part of Service-wide planning efforts, CRS managers attempt to anticipate major congressional issues. The program identifies and defines major issues, structures them for more effective scrutiny by the Congress, and provides effective, timely, and comprehensive products and services to the Congress, that usually require multi-disciplinary and interdivisional contributions. The issues chosen are national in scope, receive widespread public attention, have significant effects on the federal budget, economy, or social fabric of the Nation, and are virtually certain to be the subject of congressional hearings and legislative action.

7. Limitations

The Legislative Reorganization Act of 1970 and specific provisions in various other Acts direct and authorize CRS to provide a great range of products and services to the Congress. However, pursuant to these statutory authorities and understandings reached over time in consultation with the relevant oversight committees, the Service has developed the following policies limiting or barring certain types of assistance. When it appears that a congressional request should be declined on these policy grounds, that decision and notification to the requestor is to be made only after consultation with the appropriate division chief or the Associate Director for Policy Compliance.

a. CRS cannot prepare reports, issue briefs, seminars or undisclaimed products which are of a partisan nature or advocate bills or policies. But CRS will respond to requests for "directed writing" – statement drafts, casemaking or other disclaimed products clearly identified as prepared at the direction of the client and not for attribution as CRS analysis or opinion. In no case is excessive partisanship, incorrect factual data, moral denigration of opponents, or personal research damaging to Members permissible.

b. CRS cannot provide researched information focusing on individual Members or living former Members of Congress (other than holders of, or nominees to, federal appointive office), except at the specific request or with permission of the Member concerned.

c. Members of the CRS staff shall not appear as witnesses before committees of Congress in their capacity as CRS employees or on matters relating to their official duties without the express consent of the Director.

d. CRS does not draft bills (a function of the office of the legislative counsels), but will assist with the preparation of legislative proposals.

e. CRS cannot meet deadlines or demands that could only be met by dropping or jeopardizing the quality of responses to urgent legislative requests related to the public policy work of the Congress, but the Service will respond to all requests as rapidly as is feasible under prevailing workload conditions.

f. CRS cannot accept "rush" or priority deadlines on constituent inquiries but will respond as expeditiously as is possible without compromising the quality of responses relating to current legislative business.

g. CRS cannot undertake casework or provide translating services or briefings for constituents, but can lend assistance in responding to constituent matters, including identification of the appropriate agency or private entity to contact for further pursuit of the matter.

h. CRS cannot give personal legal or medial advice, but will assist in the provision of background information, the identification of relevant issues for further scrutiny, and advice on sources of additional assistance.

i. CRS cannot undertake scholastic or personal research for office staff, but can, on a nonpriority basis, help with bibliographic and reference services.

j. CRS assistance for former Members of Congress should be limited to use of the LaFollette Reading Room and reference centers, the hotline service, the provision of readily available information and previously prepared CRS congressional distribution products. CRS cannot undertake original research for former Members, but on a nonpriority basis responds to requests for reference services and research guidance.

k. CRS is not authorized to provide congressional offices with clerical assistance (*e.g.*, typing, duplication, maintenance of mailing lists, continuing clipping services, etc.).

l. CRS must not use its staff to index hearings or congressional document other than those prepared by the Service itself.

m. The Library of Congress is not authorized to subscribe to or lend on a regular basis current issues of periodicals and newspapers for the purpose of furnishing them regularly to individual congressional offices.

n. CRS must not use its staff to support executive or other commissions that are not funded through the Legislative Branch Appropriations Act. In those instances where Members of Congress are official members of a commission not served by CRS, the Service may supply customary assistance to the Members, but queries should be placed through the Members' offices by their official staffs, and the replies should be sent to the Members' offices, not to the office of the commission.

o. CRS does not conduct audits or field investigations.

p. CRS is not authorized to provide its services in support of political campaign organizations.

q. While CRS reference and research specialists serve all Members and committees of Congress, the director has the authority to assign staff to work temporarily for particular committees on request. In current circumstances, however, no full time assignments may be approved, and staff assigned to close support of a committee must be available to serve other clients. When staff is adequate to permit the loan of subject specialists for short periods, the director may approve formal requests without reimbursement; staff loans for periods of over 60 days must be reimbursed. No full-time assignment of staff is approved if the assignment leaves the Service unable to adequately serve the Congress.

r. As a general rule, the services of CRS are provided exclusively to the Congress and, to the extent provided by law, to other congressional support agencies. Because of the benefits derived from the exchange of information with other governmental bodies (including elected and appointed officials of foreign governments), the Service may also at the discretion of the Director exchange courtesies and services of a limited nature with such organizations, so long as such assistance benefits CRS services to Congress.

s. CRS does not provide its services to congressional member organizations and informal caucuses not funded by legislative branch appropriations but will provide its normal services to the offices of Members who belong to such entities and to formal congressional party organizations. Current lists of organizations that may place requests directly are available from the Inquiry Unit.

t. Offer services to former Members of Congress, other than providing copies of current CRS publications or limited brief reference assistance.

How to Obtain Numbered CRS Products

Numbered CRS products are available for general distribution to the Congress – Reports for Congress, Issue Briefs, Audio Briefs, and Info Packs. A list of products currently available, together with order numbers, is contained in the *Guide to CRS Products, Update, or Weekly Update.* Requests for numbered CRS products may be submitted in any of the follow ways:

1. **By phone:**   CRS Products Line 7-7132
    District and state offices should call (202) 707-7130
    Fax-on-Demand (for fax delivery on Capitol Hill of CRS Reports with Six or fewer pages 7-9943

2. **By fax:**   Fax requests to 7-6745

3. **By Internet:**   CRS Home Page at www.loc.gov/crs (Full text of all CRS products, and " products on active legislation, available online.

4. **By letter:**   Mail or fax letters to:
    Daniel P. Mulhollan, Director
    Congressional Research Service
    The Library of Congress
    Washington, D.C. 20540-7210
    (Note: Hill offices may use Inside Mail or fax letters to 7-6745)

5. **In person:**   *(Note: Hours may change when*
                     Congress is not in session.)

Library of Congress

CRS Product Distribution Center
Madison Building LM-212
Hours: Monday-Friday 8:30 a.m.-6:00 p.m.

House Research Centers

Longworth Research Center B-221
Rayburn Research Center B-335
Hours: Monday-Friday 9:00 a.m.-5:30 p.m.

Senate Research Center

Russell Senate Office Building..... SR-B07
Hours: Monday-Friday 9:00 a.m.-5:30 p.m.

How to Request Analytical or Research Services

Specific requests for legal, economic, or policy analysis, consultation with a CRS expert, or other assistance may be made in person or by phone, fax, or letter. Requests for policy analysis or other more detailed inquiries are often made by a phone call. Inquiries are promptly routed to staff knowledgeable in the area of inquiry.

1. **By telephone:** Call the Inquiry Section 7-4700
                      District and state offices should call
                      (202) 707-5700.
                      TTY Line for hearing
                      impaired.................... 7-7154
                      Hot line, for rapid telephone response to
                      factual questions................. 7-8500

2. **By fax:**   Fax requests to 7-6745

3. **By letter:**   Mail or fax letters to:
                      Daniel P. Mulhollan, Director
                      Congressional Research Center
                      The Library of Congress
                      Washington, D.C. 20540-7210
                      (Note: Hill offices may use Inside Mail
                      or fax letters to 7-6745)

4. **In person:** Requests can be dropped off at any CRS Congressional Reading Room or Research Center or the LaFollette Reading Room. *(Note: Hours may change when Congress is not in session.)*

Library of Congress

La Follette Congressional Reading Room, Madison Building, Library of Congress............... LM-202/204
Hours:
Monday-Thursday 8:30 a.m.-8:00 p.m.
Friday   8:30 a.m.-6:00 p.m.
Saturday   8:30 a.m.-5:00 p.m.
(Closed Saturdays when Congress in not in session.)

Jefferson Congressional Reading Room
(Members of Congress only)
Jefferson Building, Library of Congress.................... LJ-G05
Hours: Monday-Friday 8:30 a.m.-5:30 p.m.

B. CONGRESSIONAL BUDGET OFFICE (CBO)

The Congressional Budget Office (CBO) was created by the Congressional Budget and Impoundment Control Act of 1974. It began operating on February 24, 1975, with the appointment of its first director, Alice M. Rivlin. CBO's mission is to provide Congress with objective, timely, nonpartisan analyses needed for economic and budget decisions and with the information and estimates required for the congressional budget process. Compared with the missions of the Congress's other support agencies – the Congressional Research Service and the General Accounting Office – CBO's mandate is relatively narrow. But its subject matter gives it a broad reach, reflecting the wide array of activities that the federal budget covers and the major role the budget plays in the U.S. economy.

A substantial part of what CBO does is to support the work of the House and Senate Committees on the Budget, which were also created by the 1974 act. Those committees are in charge of the process, spelled out in the act, by which the Congress sets its own targets for the federal budget, including the overall levels of revenues and spending, the surplus or deficit that results, and the distribution of federal spending by broad functional categories. Each spring Congress adopts the end result of that process, the congressional budget plan, in the form of a concurrent resolution. The resolution imposes an overall framework and discipline on the consideration of appropriations, other spending measures, and tax legislation.

The policies and principles that have shaped the Congressional Budget Office since its inception are a key factor in its effectiveness. CBO is a professional, nonpartisan staff office; it does not make recommendations on policy. That nonpartisan stance has been instrumental in preserving the agency's reputation for professionalism and has enhanced the credibility of its products. CBO prepares independent analyses and estimates relating to the budget and the economy and presents options and alternatives for Congress to consider. It routinely discloses the assumptions and methods it uses, which enhances the general perception of its products as objective and impartial.

Some of CBO's activities are statutory tasks; others are carried out at the request of congressional committees. According to the Budget Act, CBO must give priority first to requests for services from the House and Senate Budget Committees; second, to requests from the two Appropriations Committees, the House Committee on Ways and Means, and the Senate Committee on Finance; and finally, to requests from all other congressional committees. CBO prepares various types of analyses for Congress, including cost estimates for bills that individual Members have introduced or plan to introduce. But, committee requests always take priority. CBO handles requests from individual Members only to the extent that its resources permit.

CBO's services can be grouped in four categories: helping Congress formulate a budget plan, helping it stay within that plan, helping it assess the impact of federal mandates, and helping it consider issues related to the budget and to economic policy.

1. Helping Congress Develop a Plan for the Budget

The House and Senate Committees prepare the annual congressional budget plan, drawing on the "views and estimates" of the other committees. A major part of CBO's role in that process is to prepare an annual report, which provides economic and budget projections for the next 10 years. Typically, it also includes a discussion of some current economic or budget policy issues, such as the effects of the federal deficit on economic growth or recent changes in the budget process. CBO customarily updates its economic and budget projections in the midyear.

Economic Forecasts and Projections

CBO is the only part of the legislative branch whose mandate includes making economic forecasts and projections. Its forecasts cover 18 to 24 months and involve the major economic variables – gross domestic product (GDP), unemployment, inflation, and interest rates. CBO does not attempt to forecast cyclical fluctuations in the economy more than two years ahead; instead, its longer-term projections are based on trends in the labor force, productivity, and savings.

CBO draws the information for its forecasts from the major econometric models and commercial economic forecasting services. It also relies on the advice of a distinguished panel of advisers that meets twice a year. Usually, CBO's forecasts are fairly close to the consensus of private forecasters. CBO regularly publishes an evaluation of its economic forecasting record.

Baseline Budget Projections

The purpose of CBO's budget projections is to give Congress a baseline for measuring the effects of proposed changes in tax and spending laws. The projections start with the Congress's most recent budgetary decisions and show what would happen to the federal budget if no new policy decisions were made over the projection period. The Budget Committees use the projections to develop their annual budget resolutions and directives to other committees. CBO uses them to produce cost estimates for proposed legislation and in scorekeeping tabulations.

For revenues and entitlement programs, such as Social Security or Medicare, the baseline projections generally assume that current laws will continue without change, For discretionary spending, which is controlled by annual appropriation bills, CBO bases its projections on the most recent appropriations and the statutory limits on future appropriations. For fiscal years 1998 through 2002, the Balanced Budget Act of 1997 set limits on discretionary spending, extending the limits first put in place by the Budget Enforcement Act of 1990.

Analysis of the President's Budget and Other Assistance

Each year, at the request of the Senate Committee on Appropriations, CBO analyzes the President's budget to see how its revenue and spending proposals would affect CBO's baseline budget projections. In the analysis, CBO uses its own economic assumptions and estimating techniques to recast the budget the President has proposed and submitted to the Congress. In addition, as Congress moves towards its annual budget resolution, CBO helps the budget and other committees estimate the effects of alternative budget plans. Frequently, CBO officials are asked to testify before congressional committees about the outlook for the economy and the budget and about other matters related to developing the annual budget plan.

Long-Term Budgetary Pressures and Policy Options

The 10-year time frame CBO uses for preparing budget projections is not sufficient to show the dramatic effects that the projected demographic changes in the U.S. population over the next three decades will have on the federal budget. The upcoming retirement of the large baby-boom generation and the continuing growth of per-enrollee health care costs will place growing pressure on the budget, largely because they will increase spending on Social Security, Medicare, and other programs that serve the elderly. Since 1996, CBO has prepared an annual report on the long-term budgetary outlook and on some of the policy options for controlling the growth of spending in those programs.

2. Helping the Congress Stay within its Budget Plans

Once Congress adopts the annual budget resolution, the Budget Committees take the lead in enforcing its provisions. To help them, CBO supplies estimates of the budgetary impact of bills reported by the different committees and up-to-date tabulations (referred to as scorekeeping) of the status of congressional actions on legislation that affects the budget. CBO also prepares a series of sequestration reports that advise the Congress and the administration on two matters: where the appropriation limits on discretionary spending have been exceeded, and whether the enactment of any legislation that affects direct spending or receipts has increased the budget deficit.

Cost Estimates for Bills

CBO is required to develop a cost estimate for virtually every bill reported by congressional committees to show how it would affect spending or revenues over the next five years or more. For more tax legislation, CBO uses estimates provided by the Joint Committee on Taxation, a separate congressional analytic group that works closely with the two tax-writing committees. CBO also prepares cost estimates for use in drafting bills (especially in the early stages), formulating floor amendments, and working out the final form of legislation in conference committees. To the extent that its resources permit, CBO estimates the cost of bills at the request of individual Members. In the past, where appropriate, CBO estimates contained the projected costs to state and local governments of carrying out the proposed legislation. In March 1995, enactment of the Unfunded Mandates Reform Act greatly expanded CBO's responsibilities in that area (see below).

CBO's cost estimates have become an integral part of the legislative process, and committees increasingly refer to them at every stage of drafting bills. The estimates may also have an impact on the final outcome of legislation because they are used to determine whether committees are complying with the annual budget resolutions and reconciliation instructions.

Another CBO responsibility is providing estimates to the Appropriations Committees of the Congress. The numbers contained in appropriation bills usually represent budget authority, and the resulting outlays must be estimated. (Outlays are generally checks issued by the Treasury or cash-equivalent transactions that, when subtracted from receipts, are used calculate the budget surplus or deficit.) CBO's estimates may be critical in determining whether a bill complies with allocations in the annual budget resolution and with statutory limits on discretionary appropriations.

Scorekeeping

One of CBO's most important functions is to keep trace of all spending and revenue legislation considered each year so Congress can know whether it is acting within the limits set by the annual budget resolution. CBO provides the Budget and Appropriations Committees with frequent tabulations of congressional action on both spending and revenue bills – although the bulk of CBO's scorekeeping involves spending legislation. The scorekeeping systems keeps track of all bills that affect the budget from the time they are reported out of committee to the time they are enacted into law.

Sequestration Reports

Each year, CBO prepares three sequestration reports as part of the procedure specified by the Budget Enforcement Act – and extended by the Balanced Budget Act of 1997 – for enforcing the 1990, 1993, and 1997 budget agreements between the Congress and the administration. Those reports are advisory and serve only as a benchmark for judging the accuracy of similar sequestration calculations by the Office of Management and Budget (OMB). Under the law, OMB can trigger the cancellation of budgetary resources in two circumstances: when the limits on discretionary appropriations are breached, or when direct-spending or receipt legislation increases the deficit.

In addition to the sequestration reports, the Budget Enforcement act requires CBO to notify Congress whenever it or OMB projects a recession in the next year (defined as two consecutive quarters with real economic growth of less than zero) or whenever the Department of commerce reports two consecutive quarters with real economic growth of less than one percent. If the President concurs, Congress can then elect to set aside the statutory limits on appropriations and other budget enforcement procedures.

3. Helping Congress Assess Federal Mandates

To assess better the impact of its laws on state, local, and tribal governments and the private sector, Congress passed the Unfunded Mandates Reform Act of 1995. The act amends the Congressional Budget Act to require CBO to give authorizing committees a statement about whether reported bills contain federal mandates. If the five-year direct costs of an intergovernmental or private-sector mandate exceed specified thresholds, CBO must provide an estimate of those costs (if feasible) and the basis of the estimate.

CBO's statement must also include an assessment of what funding is authorized in the bill to cover the costs of the mandates and, for intergovernmental mandates, an estimate of the appropriations needed to fund such authorizations for up to 10 years after the mandate is effective. When requested, CBO is also required to assist committees by preparing studies of legislative proposals containing federal mandates. The law took effect January 1, 1996.

4. Helping Congress Consider Budget and Economic Policy Issues

CBO's responsibilities also entail analyzing specific program and policy issues that affect the federal budget and the economy. For the most part, requests for those analyses come from the chairman or ranking minority member of a full committee or subcommittee. The leadership of either party in the House or Senate may also request CBO analysis.

The analyses cover a variety of federal activities, examining current policies, suggesting other approaches, and projecting how the alternatives would affect current programs, the federal budget, and the economy. In keeping with its nonpartisan mandate, CBO does not offer recommendations on policy in those reports.

Some of the analyses take nine to 12 months, or sometimes longer, to complete. Other analyses may be conducted in a much shorter time frame, usually appearing as papers or memorandums. Many CBO reports have helped shape public discussion of the issues they address, not only on Capitol Hill but in the nation at large. A list of CBO's recent publications shows the broad range of their subject matter.

Employing Staff and Budgetary Resources

CBO's annual appropriation limits the number of staff the agency may employ. The appropriation for fiscal year 1976 authorized 193 positions. Increases in the 1977 appropriation (to round out CBO's initial staffing) and in the appropriations for fiscal years 1979, 1983, 1986, and 1996 (to carry out additional responsibilities assigned by the Congress) brought the agency's staffing limit to the present level of 232 full-time-equivalent positions. Of those 204 are designated professional and 28 support positions.

CBO is an agency dominated by economists. All of its directors have been economists, and about 60 percent of its professional staff hold advanced degrees in either economics or public policy. Nearly all of CBO's professional staff have completed four or more years of college; three out of four have graduate degrees.

CBO's fiscal year of 1999 appropriation is $25.7 million. Of its total expenditures, the largest share – 85 percent – is allotted to personnel. The second largest component is computer costs. Today, those expenditures makes up about eight percent of total spending, but they have been as much as 28 percent.

Services and offices are conveniently located on the fourth floor of the Ford House Office Building (formerly House Annex II) at Second and D Streets, SW, in Washington, D.C. The building is served by the Blue and Orange Lines of the Washington Metrorail system; the Federal Center SW station is across from the Third Street side of the building. A shuttle bus service operated on Capitol Hill by the Architect of the Capitol serves the Ford Building.

How to Contact CBO

For general information, call the Administration and Information Division at (202) 226-2600. The fax number is (202) 226-2714. CBO is open weekdays from 9:00 a.m. to 5:30 . p.m.

How to Obtain CBO Products

Congressional Distribution. Members of Congress receive copies of all CBO reports and studies. In addition, copies of CBO papers, memorandums, cost estimates, and other analyses are available to Members on request.

Public Distribution. Single copies of CBO's reports, studies, papers, and memorandums are available to the public at no charge. Those documents are also available on CBO's Web site (*www.cbo.gov*). To request a list of publications or a specific document, call the Publications Office at (202) 226-2809 weekdays between 9:00 a.m. and 5:30 p.m. or write to the following:

CBO Publications Office
Administration and Information Division
Ford House Office Building
Second and D Streets, SW
Washington, DC 20515

To obtain multiple copies, contact the U.S. Government Printing Office, which sells many of CBO's reports and studies. For information about availability, exact costs, and ordering, call (202 275-3030 or write to the following:

Superintendent of Documents
U.S. Government Printing Office
Washington, DC 20402

CBO cost estimates are available to the public on the Web site and are generally included in Senate and House committee reports that accompany reported legislation. The Publications Office does not distribute copies of cost estimates.

C. OFFICES OF SENATE LEGAL COUNSEL AND HOUSE GENERAL COUNSEL

For over two decades the offices of Senate Legal Counsel and House General Counsel have developed parallel yet distinctly unique and independent roles as institutional legal "voices" of the two bodies they represent. Familiarity with the structure and operation of these offices and the nature of the support they may provide committees in the context of an investigative oversight proceeding is essential.

A. Senate Legal Counsel

The Office of Senate Legal Counsel[63] was created by Title VII of the Ethics in Government Act of 1978[64] "to serve the institution of congress rather than the partisan interests of one party or another."[65] The counsel and deputy counsel are appointed by the president pro tempore of the Senate upon the recommendation of the majority and minority leaders. The appointment of each is made effective by a resolution of the Senate, and each may be removed from office by a resolution of the Senate. The term of appointment of the counsel and deputy counsel is two Congresses. The appointment of the counsel and deputy counsel and the counsel's appointment of assistant senate legal counsel are required to be made without regard to political affiliation. The office is responsible to a bipartisan Joint Leadership Group, which is comprised of the majority and minority leaders, the president pro tempore, and the chairman and ranking minority member of the Committees on the Judiciary and on Rules and Administration.[66]

---

[63] A full description of the Office of Senate Legal Counsel and its work may be found in Floyd M. Riddick and Alan S. Frumin, Riddick's Senate Procedure, S.Doc. No. 28, 101st Cong., 2d Sess. 1236 (1992). For a more recent discussion of the history, development and work of both the Senate and House counsels' offices, see Charles Tiefer, The Senate and House Counsel Offices: Dilemmas of Representing in Court the Institutional Congressional Client, Law and Contemporary Problems, vol. 61: No. 2, Spring 1998:48-63.

[64] Pub.L.No. 95-520, secs. 701 et seq., 92 Stat. 1824, 1875 (1978), codified principally in 2 USC §§ 288, et seq.

[65] S.Rep.No. 95-170, 95th Cong., 2d Sess. 84 (1978).

[66] 2 U.S.C. 288(a) and (b), 288a.

The act specifies the activities of the office, two of which are of immediate interest to committee oversight concerns: representing committees of the Senate in proceedings to aid them in investigations, and advising committees and officers of the Senate.[67]

(1) Proceedings to Aid Investigations by Senate Committees

The Senate legal counsel may represent committees in proceedings to obtain evidence for Senate investigations. Two specific proceedings are authorized.

The first proceeding is under the law providing committees the authority to grant witness immunity. (18 U.S.C. § 6005). It provides that a committee or subcommittee of either house of Congress may request an immunity order from a U.S. district court when the request has been approved by the affirmative vote of two-thirds of the members of the full committee. By the same vote, a committee may direct the Senate legal counsel to represent it or any of its subcommittees in an application for an immunity order.[68]

The second proceeding involves authority under the Ethics in Government Act of 1978 which permits the Senate legal counsel to represent a committee or subcommittee of the Senate in a civil action to enforce a subpoena. Prior to the Ethics Act, subpoenas of the Senate could be enforced only through the cumbersome method of a contempt proceeding before the bar of the Senate or by a certification to the U.S. attorney and a prosecution for criminal contempt of Congress under 2 U.S.C. §§ 192, 194. The Ethics Act authorizes the Senate to enforce its subpoenas through a civil action in the U.S. District Court for the District of Columbia.[69] The House chose not to avail itself of this procedure and this enforcement method applies only to Senate subpoenas. Senate subpoenas have been enforced in several civil actions. See, for example proceedings to hold in contempt a recalcitrant witness in the impeachment proceedings against Judge Alcee L. Hastings[70] and proceedings to enforce a subpoena *duces tecum* for the production of diaries of Senator Bob Packwood.[71]

The statute details the procedure for directing the Senate legal counsel to bring a civil action to enforce a subpoena. In contrast to an application for an immunity order, which may be authorized by a committee, only the full senate by resolution may authorize an action to enforce a subpoena.[72] The Senate may not consider a resolution to direct the counsel to bring an action unless the investigating committee reports the resolution by a majority vote. The statute specifies the required contents of the committee report; among other matters, the committee must report on the extent to which the subpoenaed party has complied with the subpoena, the objections or privileges asserted by the witness, and the comparative effectiveness of a criminal and civil proceeding.[73] A significant limitation on the civil enforcement remedy is that it excludes from its coverage actions against officers or employees of the federal government acting within their official capacities, except where the

---

[67] In addition, the office is called upon to defend the Senate, its committees, officers and employees in civil litigation relating to their official responsibilities or when they have been subpoenaed to testify or to produce Senate records; and to appear for the Senate when it intervenes or appears as amicus curiae in a lawsuit to protect the powers or responsibilities of Congress.

[68] 2 U.S.C. 288b(d)(2), 288f.

[69] 28 U.S.C. 1365.

[70] See, S.Rep. No. 98, 101st Cong., 1st Sess. (1989).

[71] See, *Senate Select Committee on Ethics v. Packwood*, 845 F.Supp 17 (D.D.C. 1994), *petition for stay pending appeal denied*, 510 U.S. 1319 (1994).

[72] 2 U.S.C. 288d and 28 U.S.C. 1365.

refusal to comply is based on the assertion of a personal privilege or objection and not on a governmental privilege or objection that has been authorized by the executive branch.[74] Its reach is limited to natural persons and to entities acting or purporting to act under the color of state law.[75]

(2) Advice to committees and officers of the Senate and other duties

The Ethics act details a number of advisory functions of the Office of Senate Legal Counsel. Principal among these are the responsibility of advising Members, committees, and officers of the Senate with respect to subpoenas or requests for the withdrawal of Senate documents, and the responsibility of advising committees about their promulgation and implementation of rules and procedures for congressional investigations. The office also provides advice about legal questions that arise during the course of investigations.[76]

The act also provides that the counsel shall perform such other duties consistent with the nonpartisan purposes and limitations of Title VII as the Senate may direct.[77] Thus, in 1980, the office was used in the investigation relating to President Carter's brother, Billy, and his connection to Libya and worked under the direction of the chairman and vice-chairman of the subcommittee charged with the conduct of that investigation.[78] Members of the office have also undertaken special assignments such as the Senate's investigation of "Abscam" and other undercover activities,[79] the impeachment proceedings of Judge Harry Claiborne,[80] Judge Walter L. Nixon, Jr.,[81] and Judge Alcee L. Hastings Jr.,[82] and the confirmation hearings of Justice Clarence E. Thomas. The office was called upon to assist in the Senate's conduct of the impeachment trail of President Clinton.

In addition, the counsel's office provides information and advice to Members, officers, and employees on a wide range of legal and administrative matters relating to Senate business. Unlike the House practice, the Senate legal counsel plays no formal role in the review and issuance of subpoenas. However, since it may become involved in civil enforcement proceedings, it has welcomed the opportunity to review proposed subpoenas for form and substance prior to their issuance by committees. The Office of Senate Legal Counsel can be reached at 224-4435.

B. House General Counsel

The House general counsel has evolved in an incremental manner since the mid-1970s, from its original role as legal advisor to the clerk of the House on a range of administrative matters that fell within the jurisdiction of the clerk's office, to that of lawyer for the

---

[73] 2 U.S.C. 288d(c).
[74] See 28 U.S.C. 1365(a).
[75] Id.
[76] 2 U.S.C. 288g(a)(5) and (6).
[77] 2 U.S. 288g(c).
[78] See S.Rep. No. 1015, 96th Cong., 2d Sess. (1980).
[79] See S.Rep. No. 682, 975h Cong., 2d Sess. (1982).
[80] See S.Rep. No. 812, 99th Cong., 2d Sess. (1986).
[81] See S.Rep. No. 164, 101st Cong., 1st Sess. (1989).
[82] See S.Rep. No. 156, 101st Cong., 1st Sess. (1989).

institution. At the beginning of the 103rd Congress, it was made a separate House office, reporting directly to the Speaker, charged with the responsibility "of providing legal assistance and representation to the House."[83] While the function and role of the House general counsel and the Senate legal counsel with respect to oversight assistance to committees and protection of institutional prerogatives are similar,[84] there are significant differences that need be noted.

The general counsel, deputy general counsel and other attorneys of the office are appointed by the Speaker and serve at his pleasure.[85] The office "function[s] pursuant to the direction of the Speaker, who shall consult with a Bipartisan Legal Advisory Group," consisting of the majority leaders, majority whip, minority leader and minority whip.[86] The office has statutory authority to appear before state or federal courts in the course of performing its functions. 2 U.S.C. 130f. The office may appear as *amicus curiae* on behalf of the Speaker and the Bipartisan Legal Advisory Group in litigation involving the institutional interests of the House.[87] Where authorized by statute or resolution, the general counsel may represent the House itself in judicial proceedings.[88] The office also represents the House officers in litigation affecting the institutional interests and prerogatives of the House.[89]

Unlike the Senate, subpoenas may only be issues over the seal of the clerk of the House. In practice, committees often work closely with the general counsel in drafting subpoenas and every subpoena issued by a committee is reviewed by the office for substance and form. Committees frequently seek the advice and assistance of the general counsel in dealing with various asserted constitutional, statutory and common-law privileges,[90] in responding to executive agencies and officials that resist congressional oversight,[91] and in navigating the statutory process for obtaining a contempt citation with respect to recalcitrant witnesses.[92]

The general counsel represents the interests of House committees in judicial proceedings in a variety of circumstances. The office represents committees in federal court on applications for immunity orders pursuant to 18 U.S.C. § 6005; appears as *amicus curiae* in

---

[83] See H.Res. 5, sec. 11, 139 Cong. Rec. H5 (daily ed. Jan.5, 1993).

[84] Thus, like the Senate legal counsel, the House general counsel may be called upon to defend the House, it committees, officers, and employees in civil litigation relating to their official responsibilities, or when they have been subpoenaed to testify or to produce House records (see House Rule VIII); and to appear for the House when it intervenes or appears as amicus curiae in a lawsuit to protect the powers or responsibilities of the Congress.

[85] House Rule II(8) of the Rules of the 107th Congress.

[86] *Id.*

[87] *See, e.g., United States v. McDade,* 28 F.3d 283 (3rd Cir. 1994).

[88] See, *e.g., Department of Commerce v. U.S. House of Representatives,* 119 S. Ct. 765 (1999) (litigation in which the General Counsel was authorized by statute, P.L. No. 105-119, §209(b)(1997), to represent the House in a challenge to the legality of the Department of Commerce's plan to use statistical sampling in the 2000 Census).

[89] *See, e.g., Adams v. Clinton,* 90 F.Supp.2d 35, aff'd, 531 U.S. 940, 941 (2000); *Skaggs v. Carle,* 110 F.3d 831 (D.C. Cir. 1997); *Michel v. Anderson,* 14 F.3d 623 (D.C. Cir. 1994).

[90] *See, e.g.,* H.Rep. 105-797, *In the Matter of Representative Jay Kim,* Committee on Standards of Official Conduct, 105th Cong., 2d Sess. 84-85 (Oct. 8, 1988).

[91] See e.g., Hearing, "The Attorney General's Refusal to Provide Congressional Access to 'Privileged' Inslaw Documents," before the Subcommittee on Economic and Commercial Law, Committee on the Judiciary, 101st Cong., 2d Sess. 77-104 (Dec. 5, 1990).

[92] *See, e.g.,* 132 Cong. Rec. 3036-38 (1986) (floor consideration of contempt citation against two witnesses who refused to testify concerning alleged assistance provided to former Philippines President Ferdinand E. Marcos and his wife).

cases affecting House committee investigations;[93] defends against attempts to obtain direct or indirect judicial interference with congressional subpoenas or other investigatory authority;[94] represents committees seeking to prevent compelled disclosure of non-public information relating to their investigatory or other legislative activities;[95] and appears in court on behalf of committees seeking judicial assistance in obtaining access to documents or information, such as documents that are under seal or materials which may be protected by Rule 6(e) of the Federal Rules of Criminal Procedure.[96]

Like the Senate legal counsel's office, the House general counsel's office devotes a large portion of its time rendering informal advice to individual members and committees. Unlike its Senate counterpart, however, the general counsel will sometimes provide formal advice in the form of memorandum opinions[97] and, less commonly, testimony at hearings.[98]

Finally, the office also takes on special tasks as, for example, when a former deputy general served as special counsel to the joint committee investigating the Iran-Contra affair and played an active role in establishing procedures for the investigation. The Office can be reached at 225-9700. Its website address is http://intranet.house.gov/ogc.

D. GENERAL ACCOUNTING OFFICE (GAO)

The General Accounting Office (GAO) was established by the Budget and Accounting Act of 1921 (31 U.S.C. 702) as an independent auditor of government agencies. Over the years, Congress has expanded GAO's audit authority, added new responsibilities and duties, and strengthened GAO's ability to perform independently of the executive branch. GAO is under the control and direction of the Comptroller General of the United States, who is appointed by the President with the advice and consent of the Senate for at term of 15 years.

GAO's core values define the organization and its people. These core values are accountability, integrity, and reliability.

1. Accountability

Most GAO reviews are made in response to specific congressional requests. GAO is required to do work requested by committee chairmen and, as a matter of policy, assigns equal status to requests from ranking minority members. To the extent possible, GAO also

---

[93] *See, e.g., Dornan v. Sanchez,* 978 F.Supp. 1315, 1317 n.1 (C.D. Ca. 1997).

[94] *See, e.g., Harris v. Board of Governors,* 938 F.2d 720 (7th Cir. 1991); *United States v. United States House of Representatives,* 556 F.Supp. 150 (D.D.C. 1983).

[95] *See, e.g., United States v. McDade,* No. 96-1508 (3d Cir. July 12, 1996) (unpublished order quashing subpoenas to the Committee on Standards of Official Conduct); *Brown & Williamson Tobacco Corp. v. Williams* 62 F.3d 408 (D.C. Cir. 1995); *Pentagen Technologies Int'l, Ltd. V. Committee on Appropriations of the United States House of Representatives,* 20 F.Supp.2d 41 (D.D.C. 1998), aff'd, 194 F.3d 174 (D.C. Cir. 1998).

[96] *See, e.g., In re Harrisburg Grand Jury,* 638 F.Supp. 43 (M.D. Pa. 1986).

[97] See, e.g., 131 Cong. Rec. 25793-95 (1985)(opinion on the constitutionality of the Competition in Contracting Act.)

[98] See, *e.g.,* Hearings, "Environmental Crimes at the Rocky Flats Nuclear Facility", before the Subcommittee on Investigation and Oversight, Committee on Science, Space and Technology, 101st Cong., 2d Sess. 1645-67 (1992) (Statement of Deputy General Counsel Charles Tiefer on requiring the President to claim executive privilege.)

responds to individual member requests. Other assignments are initiated pursuant to standing commitments to congressional committees, and some reviews are specifically required by law. Finally, some assignments are independently undertaken in accordance with GAO's basic legislative responsibilities. GAO staff are located in Washington and in offices across the United States.

Types of Questions GAO Answers

- Is a federal program achieving the desired results, or are changes needed in government policies or management?

- Are there better ways of accomplishing the objectives of a federal program at lower costs?

- Is a government program being carried out in compliance with applicable laws and regulations, and are data furnished to Congress on the program accurate?

- Do opportunities exist to eliminate waste and inefficient use of public funds?

- Are funds being spent legally, and is accounting for them accurate?

2. Integrity

Integrity describes the high standards that GAO sets for itself in the conduct of its work. GAO seeks to take a professional, objective, fact-based, fair and balanced approach to all of its activities. Integrity is the foundation of its reputation and GAO's approach to its work.

Products

GAO provides oral briefings, testimony, and written reports. Written reports vary in format and content depending on the complexity of the assignment. If agreements reached during early discussions differ substantially from the original request, GAO often confirms changes in writing to ensure a mutual understanding about the assignment. Sometimes, agreements need to be altered as an assignment progresses. For example, a requester's needs may change, the required data may be unavailable or unobtainable in the time allowed, or the methodology may need to be changed. In these cases, GAO works with the requester to revise the assignment. Again, substantial changes from previous agreements are often confirmed in writing.

Early communication with the requester also is important because:

Similar or duplicate requests may be received. GAO tries to consolidate assignments and provide copies of a report to each requester.

An ongoing review may address (or may be revised to address) a requester's concerns. GAO works with the requester to ensure a satisfactory and prompt response.

A recently completed review may adequately address a requester's concerns and make starting a new assignment unnecessary.

GAO may not be the most appropriate agency to perform the assignment. In those cases, GAO will suggest referring the assignment to the congressional Budget Office, the Congressional Research Service, the inspector general of a particular agency, or the agency itself. GAO remains available to help a requester if the information provided does not meet the requester's needs.

GAO strives to use its budget and staff resources effectively. On occasion, the resources required by congressional requests exceed the supply of talent available within GAO. Also, in some cases, the GAO staff most knowledgeable of a request's subject matter are engaged on other assignments and are not immediately available. In either case, GAO will do everything possible to respond to a new congressional request. However, it may be necessary to delay starting some requests. In those cases, GAO seeks the requesters' help in setting priorities.

3. Reliability

Reliability describes GAO's goal for how its work is viewed by Congress and the American public. GAO's objective is to produce high quality reports, testimony, briefings, legal opinions, and other products and services that are timely, accurate, useful, clear, and candid.

The effectiveness of GAO products derives from their quality and the way requesters and agency officials use them to improve government operations. GAO offers a range of products to communicate the results of its work. The type of product resulting from a particular assignment depends on the assignment's objectives and/or a requester's needs. In selecting a type of product, tradeoffs may be necessary in scope, detail, or time GAO's products include written reports to Congress, committees, or individual members; testimony; and oral briefings.

4. Additional Services

In addition to its audits and evaluations, GAO offers a number of other services.

a.   Special Investigations

The GAO Office of Special Investigations conducts special investigations of alleged violations of federal criminal or civil law. Typical cases involve conflict of interest, questions of ethics, or procurement and contract fraud. These investigations examine the allegations using interviews, record examinations, and other investigative techniques. Completed investigations usually are reported in writing, but opinions and conclusions are not included. Because of the potential implications of unlawful acts or conduct, GAO must be careful to protect the rights of persons suspected of wrongdoing. Thus, investigative reports are not widely distributed.

b. **Legal Services**

GAO provides legal services, which include offering legal opinions and commenting on proposed bills. GAO adjudicates claims for and against the government and resolves bid protests on government contracts. In addition, GAO reviews and reports to Congress on proposed rescissions and deferrals of federal funds.

c. **Accounting and Financial Management Policy**

GAO prescribes accounting principles and standards for the executive branch. It also advises federal agencies on fiscal and other policies and procedures and prescribe standards for auditing government programs.

d. **Audit/Evaluation Community Support**

GAO also provides other services to help the audit and evaluation community improve and keep abreast of current developments. For example, it publishes and distributes papers on current audit and evaluation methodologies and approaches; assists in various training programs sponsored by these organizations; and sponsors an international auditor fellowship program to help other nations achieve an effective audit/evaluation organization.

e. **Committee Support**

Occasionally, GAO assigns staff to work directly for congressional committees. In these cases, the staff assigned represent a committee and not GAO.

5. Obtaining GAO Services

Congressional requesters are encouraged to contact GAO on an informal basis prior to submitting a written request. GAO staff are pleased to consult with requesters or their staffs and help them frame questions and issues and formulate strategies and approaches even before a request letter is written.

GAO encourages the continuation of close working relationship between requesters or their staffs and GAO. GAO's Office of Congressional relations (512-4400) can help requesters identify an appropriate GAO point for contact. To request formally GAO assistance, write to:

The Honorable David M. Walker
Comptroller General of the United States
441 G. Street NW
Washington, DC 20548

Information about GAO and the materials it produces can be obtained from its Worldwide Web: *www.gao.gov.*

E. Office of Management and Budget (OMB)

The Office of Management and Budget came into existence in 1970; its predecessor agency, the Bureau of the Budget, dated back to 1921. Initially established as a unit in the Treasury Department, since 1939 the budget agency has been a part of the Executive Office of the President.

1. Capabilities

a.   OMB is the *President's* agent for the management and implementation of policy, including the federal budget.

b.   OMB's *major* responsibilities include:

1.   Assisting the President in the preparation of the budget and development of a fiscal program.

2.   Supervising and controlling the administration of the budget, including transmittal to Congress of proposals for deferrals and rescissions

3.   Keeping the President informed about agencies' activities (proposed, initiated, and completed), in order to coordinate efforts, expend appropriations economically, and minimize overlap and duplication.

4.   Administering the process of review of proposed and final agency files established by Executive Order 12866.

5.   Administering the process of review and approval of collections of information by federal agencies collect, maintain, and use statistics; how agencies archives are maintained; how agencies develop systems for insuring privacy, confidentiality, security, and the sharing of information collected by the government; and how the government acquires and uses information collected by the government; and now the government acquires and uses information technology, pursuant to the Paperwork Reduction Act of 1995.

6.   Overseeing the manner in which agencies disseminate information to the public (including electronic dissemination); how agencies college, maintain, and use statistics; how agencies develop systems for insuring privacy, confidentiality, security, and the sharing of information collected by the government; and how the government acquires and uses information technology, pursuant to the Paperwork Reduction Act of 1995.

7.   Studying and promoting better governmental management, including making recommendations to agencies regarding their administrative organization and operations.

8. Helping the President by clearing and coordinating the advice of agencies regarding legislative proposals and making recommendations about presidential action on legislation.

9. Assisting in the preparation, consideration, and clearance of executive orders and proclamations.

10. Planning and developing information systems that provide the President with program performance data.

11. Establishing and overseeing implementation of financial management policies and requirements for the federal government as required by the Chief Financial Officer Act of 1990.

12. Assisting in development of regulatory reform proposals and programs for paperwork reduction, and then the implementation of these initiates.

13. Improving the economy and efficiency of the federal procurement process by providing overall direction for procurement policies, regulations, procedures, and forms.

14. Establishing policies and methods that reduce fraud, waste, and abuse, and coordinating the work of the inspectors general through the President's Counsel on Integrity and Efficiency and the Executive Council on Integrity and Efficiency.

2. Limitations

OMB is inevitably drawn into institutional and partisan struggles between the President and congress. Difficulties for Congress notwithstanding, OMB is the central clearinghouse for executive agencies and is, therefore, a rich source of information for investigative and oversight committees.

F. Budget Information

Since enactment of the 1974 Budget Act, as amended, Congress has more budgetary information than ever before. Extensive budgetary materials are also available from the executive branch. Some of them major sources of budgetary information are available on and off Capitol Hill. They include: (1) the President and executive agencies (recall that under the Budget and Accounting Act of 1921, the President presents annually a national budget to Congress; (2) the Congressional Budget Office; (3) the House and Senate Budget Committees; (4) the House and Senate Appropriations Committees; and (5) the House and Senate legislative committees. In addition, the General Accounting Office and the Congressional Research Service prepare fiscal and other relevant reports for the legislative branch.

Worth mention is that discretionary spending, the component of the budget that the Appropriations Committees oversee through the appropriations process, accounts for about one-third of federal spending. Other House and Senate committees, particularly Ways and Means and Finance, oversee more than $1 trillion in spending through reauthorizations, direct spending measures, and reconciliation legislation. In addition, Ways and Means and Finance oversee a diverse set of programs, including tax collection, tax expenditures, and some user fees, through the revenue process. The oversight activities of all of these committees is enhanced through the use of the diverse range of budgetary information that is available to them.

1. Executive Branch Budget Products

Budget of the United States Government, Fiscal Year 2002 contains the Budget Message of the President and information on the President's 2002 budget proposals by budget function.

Analytical Perspectives, Budget of the United States Government, Fiscal Year 2002 contains analyses that are designed to highlight specified subject areas or provide other significant presentations of budget data that place the budget in perspective.

The Analytical Perspectives volume includes economic and accounting analyses; information on Federal receipts and collections; analyses of federal spending; detailed information on Federal borrowing and debt; the Budget Enforcement Act preview report; current services estimates; and other technical presentations. It also includes information on the budget system and concepts and a listing of the federal programs by agency and account.

Historical Tables, Budget of the United States Government, Fiscal Year 2002 provides data on budge receipts, outlays, surpluses or deficits, federal debt, and federal employment covering an extended time period – in most cases beginning in fiscal year 1940 or earlier and ending in fiscal year 2004. These are much longer time periods than those covered by similar tables in other historical data in the budget documents have been made consistent with the concept and presentation used in the 2001 budget, so the data series are comparable over time.

Budget of the United States Government, Fiscal Year 2002 -- Appendix contains detailed information on the various appropriations and funds that constitute the budget and is designed primarily for the use of the Appropriations committee. The Appendix contains more detailed financial information on individual programs and appropriation accounts than any of the other budget documents. It includes for each agency: the proposed text of appropriations language, budget schedules for each account, new legislative proposals, explanations of the work to be performed and the funds needed, and proposed general provisions applicable to the appropriations of entire agencies or groups of agencies. Information is also provided on certain activities whose outlays are not part of the budget totals. The *Appendix* is perhaps the most useful product in the President's initial budget submission for obtaining programmatic detail.

A Citizen's Guide to the Federal Budget, Budget of the United States Government, Fiscal Year 2002 provides general information about the budget and the budget process for the general public.

Budget System and Concepts, Fiscal Year 2002 contains an explanation of the system and concepts used to formulate the President's budget proposals.

Budget Information for States, Fiscal Year 2002 in an Office of Management and Budget (OMB) publication that provides proposed state-by-state obligations for major federal formula grant programs to state and local governments. The allocations are based on the proposals in the President's budget. The report is released after the budget and can be obtained from the Publications Office of the Executive Office of the President.

Automated Sources of Budget Information. The information contained in the above-listed documents is available in electronic format from the following sources: (1) CD-ROM. The CD-ROM contains all of the budget documents and software to supporting reading, printing, and searching for documents. The CD-ROM also has many of the tables in the budget in spreadsheet format. (2) Internet. All budget documents, including documents that are released at a future date, will be available through the World Wide Web, use of the following address: *www.gpo.gov/usbudget.*

Several other points about the President's budget and executive agency budget products are worth noting. First, the President's budgetary communications to Congress continue after the January/February submission and usually include a series of budget amendments and supplementals, the Mid-Session Review, Statements of Administration Policy (SAPs) on legislation, and even revised budgets on occasion. Second most of these additional communications are issued as House documents and are available on the World Wide Web form GPO Access or the OMB homepage (in the case of SAPs). Third, the initial budget products often do not provide sufficient information on the President's budgetary recommendations to enable committees to begin developing legislation, and that further budgetary information is provided in the "justification" materials (see below) and the later submission of legislative proposals. Finally, the internal executive papers (such as agency budget submissions to OMB) often are not made available to Congress.

2. Some Other Sources of Useful Budgetary Information

a. *Committees on Appropriations.* The subcommittees of the House and Senate Appropriations Committees hold extensive hearings on the fiscal year appropriations requests of federal departments and agencies. The Appropriations Subcommittees typically print agency *justification material* with the hearing record of the federal officials concerning these requests.

   Each federal department or agency submits *justification material* to the Committees on Appropriations. Their submissions can run from several hundreds of pages to over two thousand pages.

b. *Budget Committees.* House and Senate Budget Committees, in preparing to report the annual concurrent budget resolution, conduct hearings on overall federal budget policy. These hearings and other fiscal analyses made by these panels address various aspects of federal programs and funding levels which can be useful sources of information.

c. *Other Committees.* To assist the Budget Committees in developing the concurrent budget resolution, other committees are required to prepare "views and estimates" of programs in their jurisdiction. Committee views and estimates, usually packaged together and issued as a committee print, also may be a useful source of detailed budget data.

d. *Internal Agency Studies and Budget Reviews.* These agency studies and reviews are often conducted in support of budget formulation and can yield useful information about individual programs. The budgeting documents, evaluations, and priority rankings of individual programs. The budgeting documents, evaluations, and priority rankings of individual agency programs can provide insights into executive branch views of the importance of individual programs.

G. BENEFICIARIES, PRIVATE ORGANIZATIONS, AND INTEREST GROUPS

Committees and Members can acquire useful information about executive branch programs and performance from the beneficiaries of those programs, private organizations, and interest groups. An effective oversight device, for example, is to ask beneficiaries how well federal programs and services are working. A variety of methods might be employed to solicit the views of those on the receiving end of federal programs and services, including investigations and hearings, field and on-site meetings, surveys and opinion polls, and Websites. The result of such efforts can assist committees in obtaining policy-relevant information about program performance and in evaluating the problems people might be having with federal administrators and agencies.

These are numerous think tanks, universities, or associations, for instance, that periodically conduct studies of public policy issue and advise Members and others on how well federal agencies and programs are working. Similarly, numerous interest groups are active in monitoring areas such as civil rights, education, or health and they are not reluctant to point out alleged bureaucratic failings to committees and Members. Some of these groups may also assist committees and Members in bringing about improvements in agencies and programs.

There are also scores of social, political, scientific, environmental, and humanitarian nongovernmental organizations (NGOs) located around the world. Working with governments, corporations, foundations, and other entities are such NGOs as Greenpeace, Amnesty International, the World Resources Institute, the Red Cross, and the Save the Children Fund. Many NGOs might provide valuable assistance to congressional overseers because they "do legal, scientific, technical, and policy analysis; provide services; shape, implement, monitor, and enforce national and international commitments; and change institutions and norms."[99]

---

[99] Jim Bencivenga, "Critical Mass," *Christian Science Monitor,* February 3, 2000, p. 15. Also see "NGOs," *The Economist,* January 29, 2000, pp. 25-27.

SELECTED READINGS

General

Bimber, Bruce. "Information as a Factor in Congressional Politics," Legislative Studies Quarterly, v. XVI, November 1991: 585-605.

Carnegie Commission on Science, Technology, and Government. Science, Technology, and Congress: Analysis and Advice from the Congressional Support Agencies. Washington: The Carnegie Commission, 1991. 70p.

Chubb, John E. Interest Groups and the Bureaucracy. Stanford, Calif.: Stanford University Press, 1983. 319p.

Gilmour, Robert S. and Alexis A. Halley, eds. Who Makes Public Policy? Chatham, N.J.: Chatham House Publishers, Inc., 1994. 390p.

JK585.W48

Moe, Ronald C., project coordinator. General Management laws: A Selective Compendium. CRS Report RL30795, January 8, 2001.

Heinz, John P., et al. The Hollow Core: Private Interests in National Policy Making. Cambridge, Mass.: Harvard University Press, 1993. 450p.

JK1118.H55

Symposium: Policy Analysis for Congress. Journal of Policy Analysis and Management, v. 8, Winter 1989: 1-52.

U.S. Congress. Joint Committee on the Organization of Congress. Support Agencies. Hearing before the Joint Committee on the Organization of Congress. 103rd Congress, First Session, June 10, 1993, Washington: G.P.O., 1993.

KF25.07

Weiss, Carol H. "Congressional Committees As Users of Analysis," Journal of Policy Analysis and Management, v. 8, Summer 1989: 411-431.

Congressional Research Service

Carney, Eliza Newlin. "Billington's Book Wars," National Journal, v. 24, March 21, 1992: 695-698.

Cole, John Y. "Jefferson's Legacy: A Brief History of the Library," Library of Congress Bulletin, v. 50, April 8, 1991: 124-130.

Dalrymple, Helen. "Congressional Research Service: Think Tank, Policy Consultant and Information Factory," Library of Congress Information Bulletin, v. 49, September 24, 1990: 319-326.

Gude, Gilbert. "Congressional Research Service: The Research and Information Arm of Congress," Government Information Quarterly, v. 2, January 1985: 5-11.

Robinson, William H. "The Congressional Research Service: Policy Consultant, Think Tank, and Information Factory," In Organizations for Policy Analysis: Helping Government Think. Edited by Carol H. Weiss. Newbury Park, Calif.: Sage Publications, 1992, pp. 181-200.

General Accounting Office

Abikoff, Kevin T. "The Role of the Comptroller General in Light of Bowsher v. Synar," Columbia Law Review, v. 87, November 1987: 1539-1563.

Bowsher, Charles A. "Meeting the New American Management Challenge in a Federal Agency: Lessons from the General Accounting Office," Public Administration Review, v. 52, Jan.-Feb. 1992: 3-7.

Chelimsky, Eleanor. "Expanding GAO's Evaluation Capabilities," Bureaucratic, v. 20, Spring 1991: 29-31.

Havens, Harry. "What We Were, Who We Are," GAO Journal, Winter-Spring 1990: 33-52.

Kaiser, Frederick M. General Accounting Office and Comptroller General: A Brief Overview. CRS Report RL 30349, August 22, 2000.

Mosher, Frederick C. A Tale of Two Agencies: A Comparative Analysis of the General Accounting Office and the Office of Management and Budget. Baton Rouge, La.: Louisiana State University press, 1984. 219 p.

                                                                      HJG802.M682

Rozell, Mark J. "The Role of General Accounting Office Evaluation in the Post Reform Congress: The Case of General Revenue Sharing," International Journal of Public Administration, v. 7, Sept. 1985: 267-290.

U.S. Congress. House. Committee on Government Reform and Oversight. Oversight of the General Accounting Offices High-Risk Series. 105th Congress, 1st Session. Washington: G.P.O., 1997. 114 p.

U.S. Congress. Senate. Committee on Governmental Affairs. The Roles, Mission and Operation of the U.S. General Accounting Office. Report Prepared by the National Academy of Public Administration. Senate Print 103-87, 103 Congress, 2d Session. Washington: G.P.O., 1994. 106 p.

U.S. Congress. House. Committee on Rules. Congressional Oversight: A "How-To" Series of Workshops. Committee Print. 106th Congress, 1st Session. Washington: G.P.O. 2000. See pp. 90-143.

Congressional Budget Office

A Profile of the Congressional Budget Office. Washington: Congressional Budget Office, 1990. 34p.

Collender, Stanley E. The Guide to the Federal Budget: Fiscal 2000. New York: The Century Foundation, 1999. 209 p.

Howard, James A. "Government Economic Projections: A Comparison Between CBO and OMB," Public Budgeting & Finance, v. 7, Autumn 1987: 14-25.

Keith, Robert and Allen Schick. Manual on the Federal Budget Process, CRS Report 98-720. GOV, August 28, 1998.

Schick, Allen. Congress and Money. Washington, D.C.: The Urban Institute, 1980. 604 p.

                                                            HJ2051.S34

Twogood, R. Philip. "Reconciling Politics and Budget Analysis: The Case of the Congressional Budget Office," Public Budgeting and Financial Management, v. 3, no. 1, 1991: 65-87.

Offices of Senate Legal Counsel and House General Counsel

Salokar, Rebecca Mae. "Legal Counsel for Congress: Protecting Institutional Interests," Congress and the Presidency. Vol. 20, No. 2, Autumn 1993: 131-155.

Tiefer, Charles. "The Senate and House Counsel Offices: Dilemmas of Representing in Court the Institutional Congressional Client," Law and Contemporary Problems, v. 61, Spring 1998: 48-63.

APPENDIX D

Congressional Oversight Video Series

Oversight: A Key Congressional Function. Former Representative Lee Hamilton delivered the keynote address to a 1999 series of CRS programs examining various aspects of Congressional Oversight. In this program, Mr. Hamilton emphasizes the importance of traditional oversight and reviews factors that contribute to successful oversight.
Program Length: 40:45. Program #: VB60016&AB50381.

The Constitutional Context of Oversight. Michael Stern, senior counsel with the House General Counsel's Office, and Michael Davidson, former Senate General Counsel, discuss the constitutional context of oversight. In addition, the two attorneys address a variety of oversight topics, including congressional investigations. Taped as part of a 1999 series of CRS programs examining various aspects of Congressional Oversight.
Program Length: 58:15. Program #: VB60016 & AB50381.

The "Rules & Tools" of Oversight. This program focuses on the formal institutional rules that committees must follow to insure the legitimacy and fairness of oversight proceedings. The nature of the formidable powers of inquiry available to congressional committees and the practicalities of their effective utilization are also explored. Taped as part of a 1999 series of CRS programs examining various aspects of Congressional Oversight.
Program Length: 42:37. Program #: VB60076 & AB50382.

The Role of The General Accounting Office in Oversight. Comptroller General David Walker discusses the role of the General Accounting Office in assisting the Congress in its oversight responsibilities. Taped as part of a 1999 series of CRS programs examining various aspect of Congressional Oversight. **Program Length: 42:42. Program #: Vby60022.**

Sources of Oversight Assistance. This session focuses on where congressional committees can obtain assistance in conducting oversight, especially relevant are inspectors general, chief financial officers, and Congress's own support agencies, the Congressional Budget Office, Congressional Research Service, and General Accounting Office. Taped as part of a 1999 series of CRS programs examining various aspect of Congressional Oversight. **Program Length: 43:30. Program #: VB60018 & AB50383.**

Fiscal Oversight: "Follow the Money." This seminar examines congressional oversight of fiscal and budgetary activities, focusing on the role of the House and Senate Appropriations Committees in the annual budget cycle and key support activities of the Congressional Budget Office to Congress on budgetary matters generally. Taped as part of a 1999 series of CRS programs examining various aspects of Congressional Oversight.
Program Length: 45:25. Program #: VB60019 & AB50384.

Outside Actors in the Oversight Process. This program addresses how non-congressional individuals can assist in the investigative process and in monitoring executive branch performance. The panel includes a journalist, members of public and private interest groups, and a former counsel with the House Commerce Committee, Subcommittee on Oversight and Investigations. Taped as part of a 1999 series of CRS programs examining various aspects of Congressional Oversight. **Program Length: 50:15. Program #: VB60023 & AB50386.**

Preparing for an Oversight Investigation. This program probes the "ins and outs" of how to prepare for Congressional Investigations from the perspective of both the investigator and those being investigated Taped as part of a 1999 series of CRS programs examining various aspects of Congressional Oversight. **Program Length: 59:50. Program #: VB60024 & AB50387.**

VHS copies of CRS video programs are available on loan to congressional offices. The soundtracks of many television programs are also available on audio cassettes. For the schedule of CRS Programs on Channel 6 of the House and Channel 5 of the Senate, call 7-7009. For further information about any of these programs, please call 7-7547.

INDEX